12
Characteristics
of an
Effective Teacher

"Inspirational Stories of Teachers Who Inspired Others to Become Teachers"

A Longitudinal Retrospective Qualitative Quasi-Research Study of In-Service and Pre-Service Teachers' Opinions of the Characteristics of an Effective Teacher

by
Robert J. Walker, Ed.D.

Lulu Publishing
860 Aviation Parkway, Suite 300
Morrisville, NC 27560
(919) 459-5858

Content ID: 2310077

ISBN: 978-1-4357-1528-8

Library of Congress Control Number: 2008905185

Cover photo courtesy of the U.S. Department of Education. On Cover: U.S. Secretary of Education, Margaret Spellings, assists a student with a science experiment at Venetian Hills Elementary School, a 2007 No Child Left Behind - Blue Ribbon School in Atlanta, Georgia.

Photo image at the beginning of each chapter courtesy of USA.gov. U.S. General Services Administration, Office of Citizen Services and Communications, Suite G-142, 1800 F Street, NW, Washington, DC 20405, U.S.A. The author expresses appreciation to the contributing state and federal photographers, agencies, and departments for the use of these public domain images (www.usa.gov).

Apple on book clip art image, is used by permission of Microsoft Corporation according to the copyright guidelines, © 2007, for Media Elements and Templates usages; Microsoft Cooperation, Microsoft Way, Redmond, Washington 98052-6399.

-Table of Contents-

Acknowledgments

I would like to express my appreciation to Ms. Annette Woods, Ed.S., School Psychologist in the Memphis City Schools, for her professional confirmation of this study's research findings, her valuable insights into the important role that teachers' relationships with students play in students' academic achievement, and her willingness to edit the first draft of the manuscript for this book.

Thanks to Mrs. Dana W. Vandiver, Content Manager, of University Relations at Alabama State University for her willingness to edit the final draft of the manuscript for this book.

Thanks to my student research assistant, Lakei S. Brown, for her assistance in this project.

A very special thanks to the students who contributed their essays to this book based on the consent that all assignments submitted to the academic institution would become the intellectual property of the institution and may be used for research and publication.

Dedication

As a young child growing up in the projects, in Columbus, Mississippi, while attending Hughes Elementary, I was blessed to have many wonderful public school teachers. This was back in the early sixties. Even though we received five-year-old, hand-me-down books from the white school, we had loving, dedicated teachers who made sure we learned.

My most memorable teacher was Ms. Hattie Powell, my first grade teacher. My mother was a teenage alcoholic single parent, with three children. I was the oldest. Ms. Powell, being aware of my family circumstances, cared for me as if I were her own child. Without her love and care, I doubt very seriously that I would be where I am today. In a real sense, she is my inspiration for writing this book.

Because of my mother's condition, I spent three years in the first grade. That third year, I was placed in Ms. Powell's class. As a nine-year-old in the first grade, naturally, I was the tallest student in my class. I vividly recall how I hated going out in the hall when my class would line up to go to the cafeteria or playground. Students from other classes would say, "Look at that boy! He is too old and too big to be in the first grade!"

Twenty-four years later, at the age of 33, I was in the graduation line preparing to receive my Doctorate in Education. As we waited to enter the arena for the graduation ceremony, I began a conversation with an older lady in front of me, who had returned to college to complete her bachelor's degree. She mentioned I was one of the tallest persons in our line. Thinking that I was an undergraduate student, she was surprised when I told her I was receiving my doctorate degree. She responded, "Wow! You are too young to be getting a doctorate degree!"

As she spoke those words, my mind immediately raced back to when I was in Ms. Powell's first grade class. In the first grade, I was told by peers I was too tall and too old to be in the first grade. Now, standing in the graduation line, still one of the tallest, I was told by a peer that I was too young to be receiving a doctorate degree.

My first grade teacher, Ms. Powell, treated me as her own child. She would tell me, "Robert, don't worry about what people say about you, just stay in school. Someday, your age won't matter." Her words kept me in school in spite of the ridicule I received during my elementary, middle and high school years. Thanks to her love and support—today I have four degrees (a bachelor, two masters, and a doctorate). As a college professor; training others to become teachers, I constantly remind my students, they can make a difference in the lives of children. Teachers do make a difference! Had it not been for the love of Ms. Powell, who inspired me to stay in school, I would not be where I am today—nor would the writing of this book been possible. Therefore, I dedicate this book to the memory of my first grade teacher—Ms. Hattie Powell.

Introduction

Over my collegiate teaching career, I have engaged college students in discussions and writing assignments pertaining to the outstanding characteristics of their most effective teachers. Effective was defined as that teacher who made the most significant impact on their lives. Students identified similar qualities among highly effective teachers. Based on those recurring themes, I have concluded that there are at least 12 clear characteristics of being an effective teacher. These 12 characteristics consistently affect students in positive ways.

This book is the result of a longitudinal retrospective qualitative quasi-research study of what college students, majoring in Education, in-service teachers (those currently teaching and working on an advanced degree), and pre-service teachers (those not currently teaching, and working on their bachelor's degree or alternative master's degree), said were the qualities of their most memorable teacher who encouraged them to become teachers.

The undergraduate students (pre-service teachers) in this study were working to earn their bachelor's degree in teaching and were not actually teaching at the time they wrote their essays. Most of the graduate students (in-service teachers) were already in the teaching profession and had returned to school to obtain an advance degree in Education.

Participants of the Study:

For the past 15 years, I have taught in colleges of Education, preparing students (undergraduates and graduates) for careers in the teaching profession. During this 15 year period, I have taught at seven institutions: Mobile College, Oakwood College, Calhoun Community College, Alabama A&M University, The University of Memphis, Trenholm State Technical College, and Alabama State University.

This study consisted of traditional and nontraditional students. Traditional students were defined as students living in the dorm and having their tuition paid by their parents or by way of student loans. Nontraditional students were defined as those who were living off campus, going to school, working, and in many cases; raising a family.

Demographics of the Study:

The participants of this study were students enrolled in the various courses that I taught within the past 15 years. Some of the courses were taught during the day, while others were taught at night. Those courses were: Methods of Teaching Science, Methods of Teaching Math, Method of Teaching Social Studies, Methods of Teaching Bible, Curriculum Development, Child Development, Introduction to Special Education, Problems in the Elementary School, Educational Technology, and Teaching in the Urban Setting.

These courses were taught at two private colleges, three public universities, a junior college, and a technical college. They were taught at predominately white institutions and at historically black institutions. More than 1,000 students matriculated through my undergraduate and graduate classes from across the United States, Canada, Bermuda, the Caribbean, and even a few students from Africa.

This multiplicity of educational courses over the years resulted in a diverse student population: young and old, black and white, Hispanic, those of Asian nationality, males and females. Some had a disability; some were gifted.

The participants in this study were: Early Childhood majors training to teach grades nursery to third grade (N-3), Elementary Education majors training to teach kindergarten to sixth grade (K-6), or Secondary Education majors training to teach seventh to twelfth grade (7-12).

The undergraduate students were working to earn their bachelor's degree in teaching. The graduate students were returning to earn their Master's Degree in Education, and some, their Specialist Degree.   There were also students who were working on an Alternative Master's Degree. These were students who had obtained their bachelor's degree in another field, such as Social Work, Psychology, Math, or Biology and had, after completing their bachelor's degree, decided they wanted to become a teacher. Some of the Alternative Master's degree students were in the process of a career change. They had worked in another profession and had decided they now wanted to be a teacher. At the time of writing their essays, some of these Alternative Master's degree students were already teaching using an emergency certificate.

Definition of Terms:
Effective - the teacher who was most successful in helping students to learn.

Characteristics – the special personal qualities of the teacher that enabled them to become a successful educator.

Research Instrument:
While teaching at various institutions, each semester, I asked students to write an essay about their most memorable teacher. They were asked to describe the one educator who had the greatest impact on their lives, was successful (effective) in teaching them the subject matter, was the teacher they most wanted to emulate, and was the individual who had the greatest impact on their decision to become a teacher.

The participants in this study were also asked to explain why they selected this particular teacher by giving a personal example of how that teacher inspired them. In addition, students were asked to discuss some of the special personal qualities (characteristics) of the teacher and to cite some specific examples of how the teacher displayed those personal qualities.

Data Analysis:

Over the years, students described their favorite and most memorable teacher using terms of endearment such as:

"She was always prepared."
"He was very positive."
"She had high expectation for me!"
"She was the most creative teacher I have ever had!"
"He was so fair!"
"I liked her personal touch!"
"I felt that I was a part of the class."
"She showed me compassion when my mother died."
"He was so funny!"
"She taught her class in a fun way."
"I was never bored in his class."
"He gave all the students respect and never embarrassed us in front of the class."
"She did not hold what I did against me!"
"He was the first teacher I had that admitted that he made a mistake."
"She apologized to me."

Semester after semester, and year after year, I began to see a common theme in students' essays and in class discussions of what makes a good teacher. It became evident that students were referring to the personal qualities (qualitative) of their most memorable teacher and not their academic qualification (quantitative). There was no talk about where the teacher attended school or what degree the teacher held, or whether the teacher had been awarded the "Teacher of the Year" at the school. The students only wrote and talked about the nurturing and caring qualities of the teacher who inspired them and the relationship they had with that teacher.

Undergraduate and graduate education majors were asked to write about the most influential teacher in their lives—the one teacher who had the greatest impact on their decision to become a teacher. These students were also asked, "Who was the one teacher that you would most like to emulate," and explain why?

Throughout the past 15 years, I listened to students during class discussions share stories about their most memorable teacher. I read their compositions and kept copies of their essays as qualitative data. Hearing students speak about their most memorable teachers and reading their essays convinced me that if teachers are to properly educate children, they must first build a relationship with them. Children learn best from teachers who care about them.

The essays students wrote regarding their most effective teacher demonstrated several personality traits prevalent in their favorite and most memorable teacher. Those personality traits were: (1) The teacher came to class prepared,

(2) The teacher had a positive attitude about being a teacher and her/his students, (3) The teacher had high expectations for all students, (4) The teacher was very creative in how she/he taught the class, (5) The teacher was fair in how she/he treated students and in grading, (6) The teacher displayed a personal touch with her/his students and was approachable, (7) The teacher developed a sense of belonging in the classroom; Students felt welcomed and comfortable in the classroom, (8) The teacher was able to admit mistakes when she/he made an error, (9) The teacher had a sense of humor, (10) The teacher gave respect to students and did not deliberately embarrass them, (11) The teacher was forgiving, and did not hold grudges, and (12) The teacher displayed compassion and students felt that the teacher was genuinely concerned about their problems and could relate to them.

This longitudinal retrospective qualitative quasi-research study of in-service and pre-service teachers' opinions regarding the characteristics of an effective teacher, was based on essays written by students majoring in education. As these students wrote about their most memorable teacher, a pattern emerged that led me to conclude that there are 12 identifiable personal and professional characteristics of an Effective Teacher: (1) Prepared, (2) Positive, (3) High Expectations, (4) Creative, (5) Fair, (6) Personal Touch, (7) Develops a Sense of Belonging, (8) Admits Mistakes, (9) Sense of Humor, (10) Gives Respect to Students, (11) Forgiving, and (12) Compassionate.

Significance of the Study:

The findings of this study were taken from student-written essays on the topic of their most effective teacher. Students also read their essays and discussed their most memorable teacher in class. Additionally, they shared their opinions about being an effective teacher in class discussions.

College students majoring in Education identified 12 characteristics of an effective teacher; and in turn, committed to being effective teachers themselves. Children currently in grades K-12 who are fortunate enough to be in the classroom of a teacher, who displays a majority of the 12 characteristics of an effective teacher, will truly benefit from being instructed by such an educator. As you read this book, I hope you will see the validity in these 12 characteristics of an effective teacher and seek to adopt these characteristics as your own.

Chapters Organization:

The chapters, in this book, were organized according to the characteristics that a teacher would need on the first day of school—then those that they should develop throughout the year. As a result, the chapters are outlined in the following sequence: (1) Prepared, (2) Positive, (3) High Expectations, (4) Creative, (5) Fair, (6) Personal Touch, (7) Develops a Sense of Belonging, (8) Admits Mistakes, (9) Sense of Humor, (10) Gives Respect to Students, (11) Forgiving, and (12) Compassionate.

On the first day of class, a teacher must be *Prepared,* she/he must have a *Positive* attitude, and she/he must have *High Expectations* for all students. These three characteristics must be present in the teacher prior to meeting any of her/his students. The remaining characteristics are more personal and develop over time as the teacher gets to know each child individually. In order to be *Creative,* a teacher must know what works best for that individual child. A creative activity to get one child involved may not work for another child. *Fair,* also depends on what is best for the child. What is fair for one child may be unfair for another child. The remaining characteristics: *Personal Touch, Develops a Sense of Belonging, Admits Mistakes, Sense of Humor, Gives Respect to Students, Forgiving,* and *Compassionate* are all more personal in nature. These characteristics are manifested as the teacher gets to know her/his students and develops a one-on-one relationship with them. Hopefully, this explanation gives you a better understanding of how and why the chapters are organized as they are.

A Word About the Essays in this Book:

Students have different writing styles and different ways of expressing themselves. In the editing process, I have attempted to stay true to each student's methods of self-expression. Therefore, other than correcting grammatical errors, these essays are presented as students (graduate and undergraduate) actually wrote them. In order to make each essay more reader friendly, I did, however, take the liberty of giving each essay a title based on an interesting topic discussed in the essay.

I begin each chapter by giving an explanation of the characteristic. The remainder of the chapter is dedicated to essays that give real-life examples of the characteristic being discussed. Therefore, instead of being given theoretical, textbook, examples of the 12 Characteristics of an Effective Teacher, this book provides personal experiences as they are expressed by students who shared real-life stories of teachers who actually manifested the 12 Characteristics of an Effective Teacher.

***

Research has shown that the single most important factor in determining a child's academic success is not the color of the child's skin or the child's socioeconomic status—but the character of the child's teacher (Amrein-Beardsley, A. 2007; Case, 2002).

The lives of the students, whose essays are featured in this book, were positively changed by their teachers who possessed these 12 characteristics. As a result, they were inspired to become teachers themselves. By acquiring these 12 characteristics, you too can have a positive impact on the lives of the children you teach.

Those of us who selected teaching as a profession did not do it for financial gain. We did it because we love children. For those of you who have been teaching for a number of years and are now facing the possibility of burnout, may these essays serve to rejuvenate you and remind you of the reason you chose teaching as a profession—to make a difference in the lives of children.

Characteristic #1

Prepared

Prepared - Effective teachers come to class each day ready to teach.

- ✓ They know the subject matter and are able to teach it in a way that students can learn.
- ✓ It is easy to learn in their class because they are ready for the day.
- ✓ They do not waste instructional time. They start class on time. They teach the entire class.

- ✓ Time flies in their class because students are engaged in learning (not bored, less likely to fall asleep).

Being prepared is a primary factor in being an effective teacher (Wong, 2001). The teacher knows the subject he is going to teach. He has read the material and mapped out strategies on how he will teach the material in a way that will be beneficial to all his students. He understands that students have different learning styles, and adjusts his teaching accordingly.

A prepared teacher is always learning. He is willing to participate in faculty development, gets advice from coworkers, takes additional classes, and keeps abreast of current literature and research in the field and classes that he is teaching. He joins professional organizations and subscribes to professional journals (Renard, 1999).

Teachers who are prepared take full advantage of students' learning and reduce students' misbehavior. The reason effective teachers are successful is because they have far fewer student problems and consequently are able to get their students to be more involved in learning. Being prepared is the first step in successful classroom management. Students have less time to get into trouble if they are actively engaged in learning. The learning process should begin the very moment students step foot into your classroom.

Classroom management includes all that a teacher does in organizing the classroom. It includes the arrangement of students, learning materials, space, and the use of time, so that teaching and learning can take place. Students take pleasure in a structured environment where they are able to focus on their own learning. The key is to make the classroom a structured and organized atmosphere where the emphasis is on creating an enjoyable educational experience for learning.

As a prepared teacher, you will arrive to school on time, sometimes a little early, with all the proper instructional materials prearranged (lesson plans, worksheet, hands-on activities, class schedule, agenda, etc.). By being well prepared, you can increase the quality of learning time by minimizing the transition time between academic tasks and activities.

By adopting the characteristic of being prepared, you will plan a variety of activities and in a sense, over plan by having more learning activities than you will be able to cover during the class period. You should also plan for the unexpected, such as a student who may finish an assignment early, interruptions from the office, or an emergency meeting with a parent. If a teacher assistant has to supervise the class while you are away, you should have enough learning activities to keep the class busy until you return.

It is vital that you remain organized. Being well organized has a positive effect on how your school day will run. Not only will you feel stress free, but your students will also feel at ease and will be more comfortable in your classroom. Being unorganized will cause you unnecessary stress, give you a negative attitude about teaching, cause you to have negative opinions about the children under your care, and will cause you to burn out.

Being prepared each day for class will help you develop effective classroom management. You will have a classroom in which students are on task and intensely involved with their academic work and misbehavior will be rare. The effective teacher, with the characteristic of being prepared, has the least amount of student behavior problems to handle. The ineffective teacher is constantly combating behavior problems.

The following essays were written by my college students, majoring in education, about teachers who taught them in grades K-12 and had the characteristic of being prepared.

What Would Mr. Deweese Do?
by
Sarah R. Hartman
One of my favorite teachers in elementary school was a man named Danny Deweese. Mr. Deweese was my fourth grade teacher and looking back, I realize how rare it was to have a male teacher for an elementary grade in 1982-83. I attended Fifth District Elementary in Morgantown, Kentucky.

I vividly remember going to school every day and always getting my day started as soon as the bell rang. Mr. Deweese was always prepared and he demonstrated his creativity through the various learning activities he encouraged us to participate in while in his classroom. Mr. Deweese had us participate in activities such as public speaking and role playing while learning the subject at hand. We even pretended to act out a "trial scene" while learning about government in social studies. He taught us through hands-on learning, which was unique in that it made us feel as if we owned the classroom. We all felt like the classroom belonged to us as he displayed our various projects and decorated the room with our art and presentation materials.

I never remember Mr. Deweese having to refer to a textbook, but instead he was prepared and knew every bit of the information that he would, in turn, pass on to us. As soon as we got to school, we started our day and kept going until it was time to go home. We were always busy in Mr. Deweese's class because he was enthusiastic about teaching and because he held high expectations of each and every student in his class! I literally loved school!

As I look back on my fourth grade experience, I realize how blessed I was to have had Mr. Deweese as my teacher. Having a male teacher was unique. It was very beneficial for the male students in our class who had no father around, to have Mr. Deweese's influence on them. I remember him participating in PTO meetings and school functions and using that time to really talk with the students and parents and create positive relationships with them. The way Mr. Deweese taught was also very unique. We always seemed to enjoy the subject at hand because of the way he taught the material. He used a lot of hands-on approaches which made us more confident in public speaking and created a fun learning environment.

I'm thankful for having Mr. Deweese as one of my teachers as I find myself looking back to think "what would he do?" in a certain situation. He truly blessed me with his enthusiasm, love for learning, and compassion for me as a person, and I truly believe he is one of the main reasons I am where I am today—desiring to be an educator! Thank God for wonderful teachers!

The Great Organizer
by
Carol L. Taylor

In Akron, Alabama, there is a school, Akron West Community School, in which I encountered many things and was inspired by this one teacher. This teacher was my first grade teacher and she taught all subjects. Mrs. Lewis was that well prepared teacher who molded me into becoming an elementary educator. In being prepared, she always had the class work or the things the class was going to cover that day laid out. Not only did she have that day's work laid out, but she had extra, exciting activities for us to do as well. Homework wasn't difficult because she went over at least one item on the work assigned. This taught me to be organized. Mrs. Lewis kept her desk clean, her room in order, and demanded her students keep their desks clean. She actually demonstrated the way she wanted the desk. For example, she wanted the books to the right and the folders to the left with the crayon box on top of the folders.

Mrs. Lewis' bulletin boards set the theme of what we were going to learn. For example, if we were doing to discuss the long 'ā' sound, she would put example words or pictures of the long 'ā' and have us to figure out the sound we heard in each picture or word. Also, if we were going to do addition, Mrs. Lewis would write the number sentence (2+2=4) and have different types of seeds as counters to demonstrate the answer. Furthermore, she would use the different types of seeds to introduce the science lesson, which brought in the social studies lesson. Mrs. Lewis would ask, "Where do they grow—the different types of seeds?"

Mrs. Lewis' class was never boring, was very exciting and educational. Mrs. Lewis, this well-prepared teacher, has inspired me to become fair, compassionate, creative, positive, but most of all—prepared!

Follow The Same Footsteps
by
Lakuita Holley

The most effective teacher I had in elementary school from grades K-6 was my second grade teacher. My second grade teacher was named Mrs. Cox. I attended Sunshine High School, which is located in Newbern, Alabama, where Mrs. Cox taught all subjects. Sunshine High School is very small. It goes from grades K-12. Mrs. Cox was one of my elementary school teachers that I would never forget. Mrs. Cox was a very effective teacher to me as a future educator, because she was very prepared.

Mrs. Cox exhibited this characteristic, prepared, everyday as a second grade teacher. As a student in her class, I can remember, for an example, each morning before class she would have the lesson plan for the whole day written on the board and would read it to the class. Every student knew what was going to be taught on that particular day. Mrs. Cox also kept a folder of every student. Therefore, the parents could keep up with their child's performance.

My most effective Elementary teacher was Mrs. Cox. She was prepared everyday. As a future educator, I will follow in the same footsteps and try my best to be prepared everyday as well.

Five Seconds Is Too Late
by
Jessica Quinn

The most effective teacher that I have ever had contact with was Mrs. Christina Steele. Mrs. Steele did not begin her adult life as a school teacher. She graduated from Oregon State with a master's degree and moved to Alabama. She began working at the paper mill in Prattville, Alabama, testing things and making a lot of money. She met her husband there and eventually had two children. She decided to take a huge pay cut and become a teacher so she could spend more time at home with her children.

Mrs. Steele taught most of the advanced high school science classes at Holtville High School. She taught me physical science, chemistry, and physics in the ninth, eleventh and twelfth grade. Holtville is also called Deatsville or Slapout and is located in a small community in central Alabama.

Mrs. Steele possesses many characteristics of an effective teacher, but the most important one was being prepared. I can not think of one day when she came to class unprepared. If she did, the students did not know it. Every day she began class right when the bell rang. If you where five seconds late, then you were tardy and had to go to the office to get a tardy slip. Not many people were ever late because they knew she meant business. She always had her notes prepared and organized in a binder with the transparencies that she was going to use that day. She also had many examples or demonstrations she was going to use out and sitting on the table ready for her to grab quickly to save time.

Mrs. Steele would let us know ahead of time when we were going to be going to the lab. She was very organized. I do not remember one day when she was not prepared for class and she made sure the students were too. She would have her notebook out and began teaching as soon as the bell rang. With her lessons, she usually had an example to make things more exciting. This helped the students' learning experience be more powerful and less boring.

Even though Mrs. Steele was prepared for class, some students who worked after school or stayed up late would occasionally fall asleep in her class. Mrs. Steele fixed this problem by bringing a camera to school and took pictures of the students while they were sleeping. This stopped the sleeping problem in her class.

When I was in school, I thought Mrs. Steele was a hard teacher, but now I believe that she was an effective teacher. The qualities that she possessed prove that. She really made a difference in my life by teaching the way she did.

Teriyaki Chicken
by
Demesha King

When I started going to Washington High School in Pensacola, Florida, I had a teacher named Mrs. Quinn. She was one of those teachers students always talked about. She was a math teacher. I really needed help in math, so I decided to take her class. I ended up loving the lady. Anyway, I found out later why nobody liked her, mainly it was because she gave a lot of work, and expected students to do their best.

She was always prepared for class. When you arrived in her class, she would have the next day's assignment written on the board, example problems written on the boards, extra chalk, just in case—or if a student was asked to put a problem on the board. Classroom or homework worksheets were already on our desks as we entered the classroom.

Mrs. Quinn was very serious when it came to math. When I say she was prepared, I really mean that she was prepared! Not only was she prepared for our class but she was also prepared for her after school math session that helped students pass the ACT test.

Mrs. Quinn definitely had a positive influence on me. Everytime I go home to Pensacola, Florida, I visit her at Washington High School. Sometimes, I visit her around lunchtime and bring her teriyaki chicken—her favorite meal!

Mr. Bastinado
by
James Ekundayo

The name of the teacher who had the most impact in my life was Mr. Oluyemi. Mr. Oluyemi was my 10th grade Chemistry teacher at African Church Grammar School, in Ilesha of Oyo State, Nigeria, Africa.

We had a nickname for this teacher, and the name was Mr. Bastinado. This name implies the type of punishment that a student receives for not being adequately prepared for class.

Mr. Oluyemi was always prepared for his classes. He was a no-nonsense teacher who gave me more than I expected out of his classroom. He encouraged me to be ready for whatever may come to me in that classroom.

Mr. Oluyemi was an expert in his field, namely chemistry, physics, and mathematics. I learned a great deal from his classes, and I believe that he made a big impression on me because I decided to pursue the field of the natural sciences and mathematics.

I have used the same approach in my profession as a teacher, to always be ready and prepared for my students, to have alternative methods for solving problems, and never to give up on my students.

It Made Me The Teacher I Am Today
by
Chauntella A. Brooks

Teachers have many different characteristics that make them an effective classroom teacher. The characteristic that my elementary school teacher displayed the most was being prepared. When I was in the fifth grade, my teacher's name was Mrs. Baptiste. She was from Hawaii. Mrs. Baptiste started each day in the same way.

Mrs. Baptiste had all her plans done in advance. She always made copies of the things she needed for the following week's lesson. Sometimes, she even prepared things a whole month in advance. She also had all her materials laid in baskets for the entire week. The baskets were labeled Monday through Friday. Mrs. Baptiste immediately started teaching when the morning bell rang. Every morning she developed a routine of taking attendance, juice and snack, and other miscellaneous things. She used a timer to guide her through her daily lessons. She was so prepared that it was easy for her to transition from one thing to another. Whenever there was a disturbance in the lesson such as a tornado drill, fire drill, field trip, or an assembly, she would always have her roll book in her hand.

Mrs. Baptiste was an effective teacher based upon her preparation for class. She was very organized and ready to teach everyday. I admired her preparedness and also developed some of those same techniques in my classroom. She had other characteristics that made her an effective teacher, but being prepared was what I noticed the most. I liked that special quality that Mrs. Baptiste possessed because it made me the teacher I am today.

No Free Time To Goof Off
by
Deifreda Coleman

When I was in elementary school, I was always intimidated by math. Fractions, to me, had to be the worst thing that a mathematician could have ever invented—that was until my sixth grade year in Mr. Williams' class. The one thing that made Mr. Williams stand out from other math teachers in the past was that he took the initiative to relate information to our daily lives. Not only relating it, but also giving students opportunities to voice their opinions to make sure that their thinking was on track about the topic. Mr. Williams always gave opportunities to practice. Whenever someone got stuck, he would be there to break the information down and explain how and why the common denominator was 16. He didn't just scribble an example on the board, or in lieu of writing, gave directions. He explained each step and then gave examples in class for practice.

I was always excited to go to Mr. Williams' class because I was not going to be scorned for any mistakes that I made. He would always explain if you needed extra help. I think the most helpful thing he did was to give homework with the answers, but you had to show how you got the answer. He didn't give a page full of problems but just enough to make sure that you had enough practice.

One characteristic of an effective teacher that Mr. Williams had was being prepared. There was not a day when everyone was not involved. We had no free time to goof off. Therefore, Mr. Williams' class ran smoothly everyday.

Al Bundy
by
Libra Y. Scott

I can remember when I was in the sixth grade that I had a favorite teacher, Mr. Dyer. Mr. Dyer resembled Al Bundy from the old television show, *Married With Children.* I loved that show. I thought Mr. Dyer was my favorite math teacher because he looked like Al Bundy.

Mr. Dyer came prepared to school everyday and he was very knowledgeable of the subject matter. Most of the time, he wouldn't use the textbook. One day, he taught a lesson on converting decimals to percents and percents to decimals. Before entering his class, this skill was very difficult for me to understand. Mr. Dyer told me to put the words decimal and percent together. When you look at the first letter of each word, it should say DP. DP stands for Dr. Pepper. This means to change a decimal to a percent, you must move the decimal two places to the right, in contrast, to convert a percent to a decimal, you must move the decimal point two places to the left. After learning this strategy, I was able to understand this skill.

Today, when I introduce this skill to my students, I use this strategy with them. Mr. Dyer was my favorite teacher because he knew how to teach in a way that his students could understand.

Positive

Positive – Effective teachers have an optimistic attitude about being a teacher and about their students.

- ✓ They see the glass half-full (They look on the positive side of every situation).
- ✓ They are available to students.
- ✓ They communicate with students about their progress.
- ✓ They give praise and recognition.
- ✓ They have strategies to help students be positive towards one another.

- ✓ They love teaching and would not want to do anything else.

As a teacher, having a positive attitude on a daily basis will create a positive classroom environment. In order to have a positive attitude, you must first love what you are doing. You must love being a teacher and most importantly, if you are teaching in grades K-12, you must love children. Your positive attitude will not only be displayed in your personal persona, but it will also manifest itself in your having an ongoing positive relationship with parents. More significantly, exemplifying encouragement and praise to your students is essential for your students to know you believe in their abilities.

The classroom environment you create for your students is equally important as the content you teach. This fact is true whether you are teaching preschoolers or graduate students. The environment includes the atmosphere, the standards you set as a teacher, the arrangement of furniture, learning centers, your bulletin boards, and how you decorate your room. Your classroom should say, "Welcome." It should have a sense of warmth when people step into it. All of these factors add up to create a positive environment for student learning.

Creating a positive learning environment requires teachers to make use of many different strategies in order to motivate students to learn and to maintain appropriate behavior. A positive learning environment will also cultivate in students accountability, self-respect, and responsibility.

Your behavior as a teacher will influence students' behavior and in turn influence students' learning. Therefore, it is important that you create a positive learning atmosphere. You should use positive reinforcement to encourage positive behavior. Always give positive feedback. Look for and point out positive behaviors. Praise the good and reward students for doing the right things. Don't always dwell on the negative (Haynes, p.1). Give positive feedback immediately when you notice good behavior. "Johnny, I really like the way you are sitting in your desk doing your assignment!" Catch the students doing good and praise them for this. Send positive notes home about the student's behavior. Give them, "You've been caught doing good!" passes to the principal's office.

Below are essays about educators who have mastered the art of being positive.

Teacher Extraordinaire
by
Zella R. Haywood

Upon arriving in tenth grade English class at Central High School, I was quite apprehensive. I didn't know what to expect from Mrs. Evelyn Mimms. I had heard horror stories about the way she treated her English students. I absolutely dreaded becoming one of her "victims" for that year; furthermore, I despised English with a passion. Certainly, I did not need a mean old lady like Mrs. Mimms getting on my last nerve.

Mrs. Mimms would always speak to us as we entered into the classroom and would expect us to respond courteously. Mrs. Mimms would stand by her door looking at each of us as we passed through the door of her classroom. The first day I entered, she looked at me with those glasses on the tip of her long pointy nose. "She always looked the same!" I thought to myself that she must have been a prison guard in a previous life because she looked so mean and serious. She was tall with a light complexion and her left cheek had a large dark mole that made her look "witchy." Eventually, all of the myths became null and void because Mrs. Mimms became the best English teacher I have ever had.

This lady made understanding Shakespeare a piece of cake. I remember her telling us that we would begin reading Julius Caesar. I knew that it had been too good to be true, and I knew she would get me soon. How in the world was I to understand this Shakespearean play and could not learn how to write a good essay without her bloodying the paper up to the point of death!? However, it seems as if she made Mr. Caesar come alive. We would read the pages of that play, and she would explain them so that it could relate to us. She brought out all of the life lessons that a teenager had and would ever experience. I remember walking out the room each day discussing the details of the play. We would debate why the characters were motivated to kill, sabotage, or betray one another. I would dare to say the unit on Julius Caesar was like a good daytime soap opera that unfolded everyday. My classmates and I were so involved in the lives of these characters that people actually thought we were discussing real people.

As I reminisce about this tenth grade English class, I realize Mrs. E. Mimms was an extraordinary teacher. She instilled confidence in her students and demonstrated to us that we could enjoy literature and writing. Her students were important to her, and she always showed a passion for her subject matter. After she showed us how well she liked English literature, and shared that enthusiasm with us, we became a fan of the humanities as well as a fan of the teacher.

The most difficult assignment of that Shakespearean unit was memorizing lines from the play. I was so afraid to get up in front of everyone and recite. The day before our recitation, she ended the class with one of Brutus' speeches. Mrs. Mimms told us that she had memorized those lines in eighth grade. We were stunned! Mrs. Mimms was very old in our eye-sight, and we couldn't believe she had retained that information for so long. Her recitation of that monologue was so inspirational because she not only assigned the recitation to us, but she showed us that she was capable of doing the assignment herself. My teacher did not expect me to perform a task that she had never mastered! I had so much respect for her that I went home and made sure that I was able to recite my monologue.

The next day I stood up and recited my speech, and the expression on her face was worth more than any grade she could have given me. Mrs. Evelyn Mimms was one of my life lines in pursuing a quality education. I know that Mrs. Mimms has inspired many students. She is now deceased; however, she made a very positive impression in the lives of the students that she taught. I must say she was one of the reasons I decided to become a teacher. She was a model teacher that cared enough to give me her best!

Beautiful Handwriting
by
Caklivious Hester

I was born in Columbus, Georgia, and raised in Tuskegee, Alabama, in the 1970s. I began my educational training at Lewis Adams Elementary School. I have always been a shy, reserved child. This shyness intensified when I entered the first grade. My state of shyness slowly faded away when I met Mrs. Stutts. My first grade teacher, Mrs. Stutts, was the embodiment of everything that an elementary school teacher should be. She was kind, patient, caring and had a smile that would light up the room. I remember thinking that when we left for the day, Mrs. Stutts, and all the other teachers stayed and lived at the school!

Repetition was the key to learning the alphabets and numbers. Mrs. Stutts held up flash cards, and we would have to identify the letters or numbers. Later in the year, we learned simple addition and subtraction. Addition homework consisted of single digit problems. These problems were reviewed and the class was asked for signs of understanding repeatedly. She had the most beautiful handwriting on the chalkboard. All of her letters and numbers were even and perfectly formed.

At times, Mrs. Stutts would ask us to solve math problems on the board. I felt so honored to be able to write next to her neat handwriting. She was extremely patient in teaching math, and always had encouraging words, even if we got the answer wrong. It has been many decades since the first grade, but I still remember Mrs. Stutts very fondly, and wish all first graders could have a Mrs. Stutts to start their school careers.

The Surprise Quiz
by
Lilia M. Knight

When it comes to influencing a child and making her believe in herself; my fifth grade math teacher, Mrs. Geneva Malone, certainly had it down to a science, and she oozed with positive feedback. Although I can remember several different occasions when Mrs. Malone's high expectations for her students and her positive encouraging attitude, caused me to take more pride in my work for her class. There is one occasion that stands out in my mind everytime I think back on my elementary school years.

I can remember sitting in my desk one spring school day with my head in my hands, my feet curled under me in the seat of my desk, and looking up at Mrs. Malone with my mouth wide open. She had just announced to the class that we were going to have a surprise quiz. I did not think I would do well on the quiz because I had not studied for it. Apparently, Mrs. Malone could see the concern on my face because she just looked at me and said, "Lilia, you will be fine."

I remember looking over each question when I received the test and thinking to myself "Oh, Lord!" because I knew I was about to let Mrs. Malone down, not to mention letting my grade down. During the test, Mrs. Malone kept reassuring the class that we all would do well and it seemed to me that everybody else must have been doing well because all my classmates kept getting up all around me turning their quizzes in while I was still sitting there going over the problems again and again.

Finally, I was the last person in the class to turn in my quiz. We graded the quiz during class and I was the only person in the class to make a perfect score.

I know I made that score because Mrs. Malone kept encouraging me to do my best.

Learning To Tie My Shoes
by
Derrick Burney

The positive attitude of my kindergarten teacher, Mrs. Anderson, had a huge impact on my educational success. From the first day I walked into her class at Central Park Elementary School in Birmingham, Alabama, I fell victim to her positive attitude. She welcomed me with a smile that gave me comfort and reassurance. She treated me, as well as the other students, as if we were her own children. She took time to make sure that every student understood the task at hand. She never limited her teaching to the subject matter; she related the subject matter to everyday life by incorporating positive morals and manners. She encouraged her students to think and do things independently. She was available when extra help was needed.

I remember when I was having a difficult time learning to tie my shoes and I wanted to give up, that's when Mrs. Anderson stepped in with encouraging words. She and I practiced tying my shoes everyday before and after school. She told me to "keep trying!" and "never give up!" Finally, after constant practice and patience, I learned to tie my shoes. If it were not for Mrs. Anderson's encouraging words, I may have never learned to tie my shoes.

So, as I stood at the door waiting for my third graders during my first year of teaching, I looked down at my shoes and once again I had that same anxious feeling I had in kindergarten. However, this time it was different because I now found myself in Mrs. Anderson's shoes, and I knew that there would be students waiting for me to give them those same words of encouragement.

I often reflect on my experience with Mrs. Anderson, especially when faced with adversity and I find myself asking, "What would Mrs. Anderson do?" Then I would say to myself, "Remember the lessons you learned when she taught you to tie your shoes—'Keep trying!' 'Never give up!'"

Circle Time
by
Christie Metz

Looking back on my years in school, the first teacher that comes to mind is my first grade teacher, Mrs. Jones. I will never forget the impact she had on my education. She was both a positive and a compassionate teacher. In kindergarten, when my mom dropped me off at school each morning, I chased her car not wanting to go in the school. When I got to first grade, I actually looked forward to each school day. I remember the special way Mrs. Jones greeted each and every student as they entered the classroom. She always had a smile on her face and a cheerful comment to say.

Mrs. Jones always made learning fun. The school day went by so fast because we were kept so busy. I still recall my favorite time of day, "circle time." I raced to be the first to sit next to her. However, there was one time when sitting next to her proved challenging and wasn't quite so glamorous. During circle time, we went on an imaginary picnic. Each student would tell what they were going to bring on the picnic. The next student would tell what the student before them was bringing and add to it what they were bringing and so on the story went. I was sitting on Mrs. Jones' right and the story started on her left. As you can guess, I was the last one to add to the story. I was so nervous that I would forget when it was my turn. However, that was the only time I ever remember feeling nervous in her class because she always made us comfortable. Amazingly, I was able to recite what everyone was bringing on the imaginary picnic!

I'll never forget school picture day that year. I proudly wore my pig tails, but dreaded smiling and showing my missing front teeth. Mrs. Jones gave the class a pep talk before our turn. I don't remember exactly what she said but she encouraged us to show our toothless smiles with pride. And that's exactly what I did. Unfortunately, I still hate having my picture made but my picture in first grade is my favorite and reminds me of her.

When that year ended, Mrs. Jones put a little note in my report card. She probably put the same message in everyone's, but I cherished mine. After all these years, I have kept the note in my baby book as a reminder of my first year memories with Mrs. Jones. Oddly enough, I am a first grade teacher, and hope that I will leave a lasting impression on my students like Mrs. Jones did on me.

An Answer To My Prayers
by
Janet Ellis

During the last several years, many articles and news stories have been produced indicating the results of having and living with a positive attitude. The late Norman Vincent Peale devoted an entire book to this issue in *The Power of Positive Thinking*. I have been very fortunate in my life to be surrounded by positive thinking people. My parents have always been positive thinkers and I believe this has benefited me well. In reflecting on my years as a school student, one teacher, Mallie Harris, used her positive attitude to affect me in a deep way.

Mrs. Harris was my third grade teacher at Cahaba Heights Community School in a suburb outside of Birmingham, Alabama. My school was fairly large for that day, having four classes per grade. Our parents were discouraged from requesting certain teachers, so the summer prior to third grade; we spent hours praying that I would be assigned to Mrs. Harris' class. You see, Mrs. Harris was well known in the community for being an excellent teacher, as well as a wonderful person. Thankfully, our prayers were answered and on the first day of third grade, in 1973, I took my seat in Mrs. Harris' class.

From the first day of school, each student in our class was told that they were each individuals that would someday make a difference in the adult world. Mrs. Harris made a point of meeting each student where we were. Our class makeup was no different than the classroom of today. We had high achieving, average and low achieving students. But to Mrs. Harris, each was a success waiting to happen.

I was one of the lucky ones who was high achieving. For the high achievers, she was always prepared with extra activities to keep us intrigued. She pushed me to be all that I could be. It was not uncommon for Mrs. Harris to call me forward during work time for her to pass along a 5th or 6th grade reading level book to me. She made me feel like I was the smartest girl on earth, and that she was personally choosing books for me.

A strong line of communication was established with each parent and Mrs. Harris. She felt involving the parents would lead to the overall success of her students. For that, Mrs. Harris gained deep respect from the adults in the community.

Math, in those days, I must admit could have sure been boring. I remember the days of listening to timed multiplication tests played on record albums. Oh, how we dreaded those tests coming. But Mrs. Harris always rewarded the class for this time by playing math games when test time was over. She turned, what could have been a truly negative experience into a positive time, even one we looked forward to.

Leaving third grade was not something I looked forward to occurring. But when I started the next year in fourth grade, I could always count on Mrs. Harris' smiling upbeat attitude greeting me in the hallway. She would ask what I was reading; indicating to me that she still cared and still was pushing me to succeed.

Through the years, I never lost touch with Mrs. Harris. After moving on to junior high and then to high school, our paths would occasionally cross. She made a point of seeking me out at community events to see how I was doing. I'd like to think that I was that "special" student who was the only recipient of this attention, but I know that's wrong. I cannot tell you how many other of her past students had similar recollections as mine.

Sadly, five years ago, Mrs. Harris was diagnosed with Alzheimer's disease. What a shame it is to think that she is no longer capable of passing on her positive attitude effect to young minds. However, what a legacy she has left with so many fortunate students such as myself. As I continue my life as a teacher, I am reminded often of the power Mrs. Harris' positive attitude had on me. I can only hope I put forth that positive attitude effect in my classroom.

Math Phobia
by
Fredric P. Daffin

Have you ever had one specific thing that you literally despised or could not understand? You did not like doing or trying to do it. Math was a subject for many years that I either ran from or reluctantly did. For many years, I was afraid of math. I never thought that I would be able to do any complex math. Then in my sophomore year of college, the Fall of 1998, God sent this wonderful woman into my life. She exposed me to the fact that I was not dumb and I could do math, but I needed proper teaching.

I had a really bad background in math in high school. Back when I was in elementary school, I really had a love for math, but Algebra 1 really turned me against math. I tell people all the time that when they introduced me to a math problem with a letter in it, they have lost me instantly.

In high school, I had an algebra teacher who would write and explain only the examples from the book on the board. She did not give any extra examples so if you did not get it instantly, you were in trouble. I have always thought that I was smart, but I just believed that I was totally dumb when it came to doing math until the semester that I met one of the world's best math teachers.

Ms. Moths would take time to explain the problems step-by-step and surprisingly, I could understand them. She finally helped me to understand the different properties. The math problems that had seemed like a foreign language for so long were now becoming translatable; This was all due to Ms. Moths' positive attitude. She always found time to show me how to do any problem that I had trouble with. She would either do this during class, right after class, or when she was in the math lab. Ms. Moths would always tell me to try and when I listened, I would always succeed. I am so thankful for her, because - since that semester, I have never again been afraid of math. Thus, I believe that this ultimately contributed to me being a positive teacher for my students.

Just Twenty Minutes A Day
by
Robin Montgomery

Mrs. Martha Duggan was my fifth grade reading teacher at Indian Springs Elementary. Mrs. Duggan was a remarkable reading teacher. She displayed her passion for reading daily. Mrs. Duggan's positive attitude gave my classmates and me the courage to excel in reading. This fifth grade teacher made reading books a pastime favorite. Books in her class seemed to come to life. She incorporated real life experiences into many books.

Mrs. Duggan made herself available. She communicated her expectations daily. I recall her always saying, "Twenty minutes a day. Just twenty minutes a day is all you have to do to become an exceptional reader!" I knew what was expected of me in her class. Mrs. Duggan used this saying as a strategy to get my classmates and me to read. It is through this persistent encouragement that I turned to a subject that I had once feared. It was in this class and with this teacher that I was introduced to a world that I had once ignored.

Mrs. Duggan exposed me to something that had not been important to me. In fact, she opened up a world of opportunities. Through her positive feedback, I was able to conquer my fear of reading. It was Mrs. Duggan who gave me the tools needed to excel in various educational realms. For this wonderful experience, I am truly appreciative. Today, as a paraprofessional and future teacher, I often find myself telling students, "Just twenty minutes a day, that's all you have to do to become an exceptional reader."

Animal Neck Ties
by
Roneshia Brown

I attended Little Egg Harbour Elementary School, which is in Tuckerton, New Jersey. Mr. Young was my fourth grade science teacher, and I thought that he was awesome.

He always seemed to start class with an uplifted attitude. He would start each class off by saying, "Hello" and "Good afternoon" in a distinct voice. After that, he would introduce his lesson and explain what we were going to do for lab that day. He was always upbeat and energetic while he explained everything. He made learning science fun and very interesting. Mr. Young had a passion for teaching that was apparent through the way that he spoke, his attitude, and his facial expressions. He always made sure that his students understood how to do the class and lab assignments.

Mr. Young always dressed neatly and professionally. On some occasions, he would wear an animal tie which would coincide with the lesson plan for the day. Everyone thought that it was so cool when he did that.

Mr. Young was also a promoter of class participation, and encouraged everyone to take a chance at answering questions during class. Whenever a student answered a question incorrectly he would state the correct answer, but he would do it in a way that wouldn't make the student feel stupid. He made every moment a pleasant learning experience. He just always seemed to know the right words to say. When a student answered a question incorrectly, he would come back to them later on in class and ask a question that he knew the student would know. This was a great confidence boosting technique.

There are several reasons why I feel that Mr. Young was an effective teacher. I remember one day when I took a test in his class and I really didn't feel good about the results. Before I left class he asked me how I did. I said that I didn't know, but I studied and did my best. He told me that it wasn't the end of the world, and to look on the bright side of things. He stated that it was just a test, and even if I didn't do that great, I could always do better on the next test. Mr. Young showed the characteristic of being positive, which encouraged me to be positive about those types of situations. He returned my test paper the next day and there was a big 'B' written on the top. He patted me on my back and told me that I did a good job, and that he knew that I could do it all along. I knew from that day on that Mr. Young believed in me.

Favorite Niece's Grandson
by
Cassandra Holley

My third grade teacher, Mrs. Flora Thomas, was the nicest and sweetest lady on earth. Being in Mrs. Thomas' class was like the best thing for me. She was an excellent role model in the profession of teaching and as a lady. Mrs. Thomas never raised her voice at us and she always treated us the same. We lived in a small town where everybody went to school together no matter what your socio-economic background was or your race.

One day in her class, I forgot my snack and juice money. Mrs. Thomas did not ask me any questions as to why I didn't have my money. She just went inside her purse, took out the money and paid my snack and juice for the week—not just for that day! The next day, I tried to pay her back the money I owed, but she refused it.

Mrs. Thomas is still the same lady I met in third grade years ago. Everytime I go to my hometown, I always make a trip to her house to visit. She tells me all the time that she knew that I would become an educator due to the way I carried myself in her class. When I go to visit Mrs. Thomas now, it is for family gatherings. I married her favorite niece's grandson.

Smart Pills
by
Meredith Marshall

My most effective teacher was Mrs. Sharon Tucker. She was my fourth grade teacher at Trinity Presbyterian School in Montgomery, Alabama. She taught me all subjects except for music and physical education. There are many characteristics that made Mrs. Tucker an effective teacher. However, there was one that truly described Mrs. Tucker, and that is positive.

Mrs. Tucker was always available to her students. For example, when I was having trouble in math, she would come early to school or stay late after school so that she could help me understand. I remember during SAT testing I would always get really upset during the test. She would come over to me and encourage me to never give up. She encouraged me to do my best.

One way she would praise me is by giving out smart pills if I answered a question right in class or for showing good behavior. Smart pills were either M&M's or Skittles in a container located in front of the classroom. I always wanted to be paying attention so that I could answer a question in class. I would do anything to receive a smart pill. For example, in fourth grade we had to learn Alabama History. I remember Mrs. Tucker telling the class that if we would stand up in front of the class and sing Alabama's state song, we would receive ten smart pills. I just couldn't wait to get up and sing

Mrs. Tucker was always positive towards me. Even when I didn't think I could do something, she showed me that I could. She communicated with me and let me know how I was doing in her class. I am very thankful for Mrs. Tucker's positive teaching ability. It is because of Mrs. Tucker that I wanted to become a teacher. I am grateful to have been given such a positive role model when I was in school.

You Are Not Smart Enough To Handle Algebra
by
Pamela Davis

> *As expressed in this essay, the teacher that leaves the lasting impact on a student, at times, may not be the most positive teacher. Out of professional courtesy, I have elected to use only the initials of the teacher's name.*

Over the years I have encountered many wonderful teachers. Some old, some young, some short, some tall, some like mothers, some sweet and some not so sweet. Nonetheless, if I had to choose my most effective teacher it would be Mrs. J. D. She was my sixth grade teacher at Catoma Elementary, Catoma is a small school located in Montgomery, Alabama. Mrs. J. D. was not my best teacher; however, she was my biggest motivator with a twist. She helped bring out my natural born tenacity. She displayed the characteristic opposite of positive.

When you think of an effective positive teacher, you tend to associate them with saying positive things to the students. Perhaps they would say things such as, "You will do well in seventh grade" or "Continue to study and practice over the summer." Instead she said something to me that gave me life-long motivation. She told me that I should not take Algebra in junior high school.

As I began to ponder over what she said, I began to translate that in plain language (language that a sixth grade student could understand). The final translation was, "You are not smart enough to handle Algebra." Knowing all along throughout the academic school year I had been practicing with my aunt and uncle who were certified math teachers and adjunct college instructors, I knew what I was capable of—contrary to what Mrs. J. D. believed. Perhaps she was referring to my California Achievement Test (CAT) results, or maybe my performance on other tests, or my race.

Whatever the case was, I was determined to prove Mrs. J. D. wrong. Consequently, in seventh grade, I enrolled in the Pre-Algebra class and passed. In the eighth grade I took Algebra I, in the ninth grade Algebra II, in the tenth grade Geometry, and by the eleventh grade, I was taking a special math called Analysis. Now, who said I should not take Algebra? Mrs. J. D.'s comment that was with negative intent was transformed into something positive. As a result, Mrs. J. D. became my most effective teacher.

Throughout my life as I face certain challenges, I reflect back upon the words that Mrs. J. D. told me — "You can't!"

I do believe what you say to children can be a self-fulfilling prophecy. For this reason, it is my sincere goal to maintain a positive environment at all times in my classroom. I try to encourage all my students to do their best at all times. We celebrate small successes as well as large successes in academic achievement. In my view, all children can learn and be successful. The catch may be that some may take longer than others. Thank you, Mrs. J. D. for telling me, I can't!

Writing Back To Us
by
Tara Bailey

As I look back on my days in school, I think about all my teachers that I had throughout, but only one really sticks in my mind. Her name was Ms. Katherine Sparks and she taught third grade at Tyndall Elementary School in Panama City, Florida. Ms. Sparks had a very positive attitude toward me and about school. See, this was my second year in third grade. My parents held me back and I was not happy about it nor did I like school. Ms. Sparks told my parents, "Let me have her and I will change all that."

Her positive outlook on me gave me the strength and the esteem I needed to get through school. There would be days that I would get so frustrated at myself that I would blow up. She would wait until everyone was gone or take me aside and talk to me. There would be many days that she would stay in and help me because I just didn't understand the concept. She would find different ways to explain it to me. Sometimes she would pair me up with a buddy to help me understand things.

Another thing Ms. Sparks did was to write back to us. We kept daily journals in her room. She always found time to write back. Yes, she would correct our work, but she always found something nice to say about it. Ms. Sparks let me see that school can be fun as long as you look at it with a positive attitude and just try.

The Day I Became Tallulah Bankhead
by
Alice Hill

As teachers, we have the ability to change our students drastically by making one decision. As I look back over my elementary years, one stands out among the rest. My fourth grade teacher, Mrs. Mathers, at Saint James School in

Montgomery, Alabama, was responsible for making me the person I am today. She took a personal interest in my life. I felt like she really cared about me as a person. She could see things in her students which they could not see themselves. At the end of the year, the fourth grade presented an Alabama History play. Several parts were added that year, one of which was Tallulah Bankhead, a film actor from the 1930s and 1940s. Up until this point in the year, I was a quiet teacher-pleaser. However, Mrs. Mathers must have seen a spark in me which even I did not realize existed. She assigned me the part of Tallulah Bankhead. I remember her telling me she thought I was perfect for the part and knew I could pull it off, even though I was shy and quiet.

When I learned that I was going to play Tallulah, I was happy, but did not realize what a profound effect it would have on me. The day of the play arrived and I was naturally nervous. I was wearing a long white dress, an oversized white hat and my grandmother's costume jewelry. As I approached the microphone, hints of butterflies still fluttered in my stomach. But, I remembered what Mrs. Mathers had said, and I opened my mouth to speak.

In a very dramatic, deep voice, I uttered the words, "Hello darrrrling. My name is Tallulah Bankhead." The crowd went wild clapping, cheering, and laughing. I even received a standing ovation.

I vividly remember how I felt. I can recall immediately saying to myself, "I have got to have more of this!" From that moment on, I was a changed person. If you ask my parents when I broke out of my shell, they will both say, "The day she became Tallulah Bankhead."

I am forever grateful to Mrs. Mathers. She could see in me what I could not see in myself. She knew I just needed a little push to break out of my shell. I recently had the opportunity to thank her for the difference she made in me. It was wonderful to tell her how much I appreciated what she did.

Renewing My Strength
by
Andrew Roberts

In today's society, education is a privilege. Many people, worldwide, are beginning to realize how important it is to possess an education. The possession of a good education comes from dedication and desire, but most of all from a good educator. Good educators are like an endangered species or a unique fossil because they are extremely rare and hard to find.

One educator who truly touched and influenced my life was Mr. John Terell. Mr. Terell possessed the characteristic of being extremely positive about his students' success. Mr. Terell was constantly reinforcing his beliefs in my ability and my beliefs in my ability. I remember once failing a test horribly and Mr. Terell said in a very convincing and sincere tone, "I know you're not going to let this test beat you. I know you've been studying because I can see it in your attitude. All this tells me is that you need to study a little harder, apply yourself, and concentrate more."

When he spoke those words to me, I felt like he saw something in my ability that I didn't see. Now I'm sure it doesn't seem like much, but he spoke these words with such conviction that it renewed my strength and gave me new courage in my ability. When Mr. Terell spoke, it was inspirational because he spoke with a type of sincere certainty. The mannerisms he possessed and this positive aura he carried seemed to be contagious. Mr. Terell has won "Teacher of the Year" numerous times, and many of his students have benefited from his optimism.

High Expectations

High Expectations: Effective teachers do not set limits on any students and believed they all can be successful.

- ✓ They have the highest standards.
- ✓ They consistently challenge students to do their best.
- ✓ They are caring professionals who build students' confidence and teach students to believe in themselves.

As an educator, you should always expect the best from your students and encourage them to learn to their fullest potential. Your expectations of your students will greatly influence their success in your classroom and in their lives (Wong, 2001). Whatever you expect from your students is what your students will give you. If you expect great things, you will get great things. If you expect nothing, you will get nothing. If you believe a child is a below average, slow learner, the child will perform as such because even if you don't say it, you will transmit these feelings to a child in your actions. The same is true if you believe that a child is a high-ability, above average, competent learner—the student will perform as such.

As a teacher, it is vital that you exhibit high expectations toward all students. Not only will it be a benefit to the student, it will also be a benefit to you. If a child believes that you believe in him, he will be more respectful toward you and will cause fewer discipline problems in your classroom.

A teacher who has the characteristic of high expectations can wield a profound influence on students (Gazin, 2004). The following essays are perfect examples of this fact.

There Is No Such Word As "Stuff"
by
Holley C. Tullis

I think teaching is indeed a hard job. But being an effective teacher is an even harder job! I never understood this concept fully until I started teaching myself. Although I had aspirations of being a great teacher, I never really understood how hard teachers had to work behind the scenes in order to pull off whatever task they were trying to accomplish until I started teaching myself. Not only does it take dedication and aspiration—it takes patience, love, care, and a positive attitude.

One of the most effective teachers I had was Mrs. Lelia Horry (mother of basketball superstar, Robert Horry who played for the Houston Rockets, Phoenix Suns, Los Angeles Lakers, and San Antonio Spurs). She taught me in a self-contained fourth grade classroom at Southside Elementary School in Evergreen, Alabama. Even though we were young, Mrs. Horry made us accountable for our own progress and success. She would often say there is no such word as "stuff" or you can't start a sentence with the word "because." What a profound effect such lessons had on us as fourth graders—had on me as a high school student—had on me as a college student—and now has on me as a teacher!!

This brings me to what made Mrs. Horry an effective teacher; it was the fact that she had high expectations for each of her students. As mentioned above, she communicated with us on a personal level that let us know that she truly cared about each of us and wanted the best for all of us. She would say, "Now Tullis, you know I'm not going to take this paper because I know you didn't do your best. Now take this back, and when you feel as if you have done your best, give it back to me." She would usually end her spill by saying, "Girrrrl have some pride!!!"

Like I said before, Mrs. Horry's teaching style had a profound effect on my life both as a student and as a teacher. I didn't rush to get through with her assignments because I knew if they didn't pass "the standards" she set for me, she simply was not going to take them. If she thought I could do better—boy, she was going to let me know it!! This in turn caused me to learn how to set those same types of standards for my own personal life. As a result of Mrs. Horry being a truly effective teaching, I, to this day, take time to do my best work and to take pride in doing my best—whatever the task!!

You Don't Have To Be A Thug
by
Reginald Bradford

A characteristic that a highly effective teacher must have is high expectations. A teacher that I remember who was a highly effective teacher was my 6th grade music teacher. Mr. Carlton Wright was his name. He really pushed me. He saw something in me that I really didn't see in myself. The lesson I learned from being in his class is that you do not have to be a "thug" or be in a gang to stand out as a young male. I learned in his class that to be a positive male you can handle your business (academics) and be cool at the same time. I had never had a male teacher up to this point. He was my first teacher who looked like me. I saw that I could be better from the way he came to work everyday prepared and ready to do whatever he needed to do to get the best out of his students. The things that he taught me in the 6th grade are the things that allowed me to go on to college and basically have to pay nothing to attend college through my music scholarship. The work habits that he instilled in me are the same characteristics that motivated me to want to teach. He taught me that you never quit. You never give up. If you don't know it, go learn it! If you don't have it, go get it! (legally of course).

There were times when I would miss notes. He would pull me to the side and explain to me that I have to practice and be diligent to be good at my craft. He told me back then that I could be a leader and a teacher. I really didn't see it back then. As I continued to work, I started to see it. To this day, I still hold Mr. Wright high in my heart as one of the people who helped me to make it.

Always On My Mind
by
Tawana Bemus

While in elementary, I attended a private school and my teacher was a nun by the name of Sister Betty. At the time, I felt that she was being hard and mean. In her classroom, there were very strict rules. For some odd reason, she was exceptionally hard on me. She would always yell at me when I wanted to give up. She also expected me to earn really good grades. She was an awesome teacher in the way that she would teach a lesson.

I remember when I was in high school, I wanted to get in contact with the teacher who really pushed me to succeed in school—Sister Betty. I discovered that she had become very ill and was in the hospital. So I went to visit her and later sent her a card to let her know how much I appreciated her.

When I graduated from high school, Sister Betty sent a card back to me with all of my pictures from the first grade. She also attached a little note to remind me of all of her expectations that she wanted me to continue to do. She also told me that she always believed in me and that she was hard on me for a reason.

When I look back, I really needed that because she motivated me to go into the field of education. By observing Sister Betty's teaching techniques, there are some attributes that I liked. I really liked the fact that she had high expectations for her students and that she challenged them. She will be one of those teachers who will always be on my mind while I am in the classroom.

The Long, Black Leather Strap
by
Petra Leonard

I grew up in a house with a working mother and two socially conscious teenage sisters. Needless to say, there wasn't much time spent with me working on academics. I can remember receiving homework and not being able to make any sense of it, mainly because I couldn't read the writing on the paper. It wasn't until I was in third grade that I began to receive help with my studies and I attribute the instruction that I received from my third grade teacher, Ms. Jones (that is if you would call what I received instruction), to my decision of becoming a schoolteacher. Ms. Jones had this long, black leather strap. I can't remember the name of the strap, but I do remember that it hurt like h-ll!!! How do I know this? Well, because I was introduced to it on one occasion. Ms. Jones would call on each student to read, and if you didn't know how to read, she thought that you weren't paying attention or was acting silly. She didn't understand that there was a possibility that a student couldn't read. Therefore, this was my incentive to ask Ms. Jones for additional help with my reading because I had had enough of the long, black leather strap.

Ms. Jones became my second mother. We would spend more time together at school reading than I would spend at home with my mother. It wasn't because my mother didn't love me, instead it was because she was a single parent with three daughters and she needed to work. It was good for me that I had a teacher (as mean as I thought she was) who was committed to her students. She always made me feel like I was the only student in the class and she constantly provided me with praise and support. I continued to progress throughout third grade and I can remember Ms. Jones saying she saw a big improvement in my reading. From that point on, I wasn't just doing my best for me, I was doing my best for Ms. Jones because I didn't want her to feel that her hard work went to waste.

There Was No Such Thing As, "I Can't"
by
Leticia Whiting

I enjoyed my elementary years because of this one teacher who I had to learn to like. My second grade teacher was the best. She was a full figured woman who didn't take any mess. I wouldn't say she was mean, but she loved her job and handled it pretty well. Every child in the school was her student. If she saw someone who was misbehaving, she would address the issue right then and there. I loved Ms. Jackson as a mother figure. She was not just my teacher. She was a counselor, instructor, motivator, and most of all—a caring person.

Ms. Jackson believed that every student has the ability to do anything they put their minds to. She believed every child could learn.

One thing that she hated for her students to say was, "I can't." To her, there was no such thing as, "I can't." She would say, "Whatever you put your mind to, it can be done." She expected for all her students to do well, and have fun doing it.

One example I would use would be when a student in another class was on the verge of being held back because of low grades. Many of the other teachers began to believe that he couldn't learn. Ms. Jackson worked with the student before and after school, so that he could get caught up with the other students. It was not easy because it had already been instilled in the child that he couldn't learn.

That student now is my closest friend who has a Bachelor of Science degree in Accounting and is doing well. Ms. Jackson played a big role in a lot of students' lives, and even though she recently retired, she will never be forgotten.

Canterbury Tales
by
Sonya B. Wilson

My favorite teacher was Ms. Vivian LaPread of Tuskegee Institute High School, in Tuskegee, Alabama. Ms. Vivian LaPread was my 12th grade English Literature teacher. She displayed high expectations for her students.

In addition to teaching English Literature, she was sponsor of the Literary Art Guild at Tuskegee Institute High School. She felt that we as African American students should know more about English Literature than vowels, sentences and etc. We were introduced to Shakespeare's sonnets, Middle English and Poetry. We were pushed to levels beyond ourselves. We read Canterbury Tales, Hamlet, Macbeth, Guhunn, and Emily Dickerson. Ms. LaPread was an excellent teacher. Ms. Lapread made sure every student learned.

"You can do anything you put your mind too," she would always say. She challenged you to use your mind beyond what you thought you knew. She exposed you to different languages and information. She made sure you knew what you needed to know about English Literature. The entire class had to learn the Canterbury Tales in Middle English in six to eight weeks and had to stand in front of the class and recite the tale. I had never heard of Middle English, let alone spoke it.

In conclusion, an effective teacher in one who makes a lasting impression on their students; a teacher that the students talk about constantly, even after graduating. These are the teachers we need today—teachers who are concerned about you learning and being happy and proud to teach you. Ms. Vivian LaPread was that kind of teacher.

Nothing Less Than Your Best
by
Vonnametre Howard

My most memorable teacher was Mrs. Mary Williams. She taught sixth grade at Trinity Lutheran. This was a small private school and Mrs. Williams believed in a disciplined style of learning. Her stature alone was intimidating. Along with the voice to match, she was the most dreaded teacher in the school. As with any strict teacher, Mrs. Williams had a bad reputation. However, even with the reputation, she managed to be one of my favorite teachers only after I passed her class.

I would say Mrs. Williams was an effective teacher because she believed in having respect and setting high expectations. Each of her students would leave her class with the satisfaction of knowing that they truly worked to their highest potential. She made sure that you knew your academic subjects. Her main focus was math, language arts, and reading. As one can imagine, discipline was never a problem. Nothing was allowed to slip through. Unacceptable work was returned and she expected it to be redone. She used to always say, "Nothing less than your best." This was expected in academics and behavior. She made it perfectly clear that attitudes had no place in her classroom. We knew she cared about us and our success. When the students were rewarded, we knew that we deserved and earned it. Now that I am an educator, I can appreciate the disciplined style she used in her classroom. I believe that her high expectations made the students have high expectations for themselves.

Aiming High for Our Goals
by
Brandy T. Howard

I attended Alfred D. Khon Elementary School on the south side of Chicago, Illinois. Mrs. Shannon was my fifth grade teacher. She was a self contained teacher whose specialty was reading. Mrs. Shannon was the kind of teacher who really cared about her students' achievements and their well being, which made her an exceptional teacher.

Mrs. Shannon would do anything for her students, and she made us feel very special and loved. Mrs. Shannon always had high expectations of her students. She never allowed us to give up. The theme for our class was, "Aiming High for Our Goals" and the number one rule was, "Never Say What You Can't Do."

If you were in Mrs. Shannon's class, you were in for a real treat. Everyday was like an adventure. On Thursday's we would compete in Math Mania. Math Mania was a class activity that consisted of two teams competing to answer math problems the fastest. On Fridays we would enjoy class Spelling Bees. Everyday we would read stories from different children's books. When a student didn't know or stumbled over a word, Mrs. Shannon would tell the student to "take your time and sound it out." She was always very patient with us.

Because of Mrs. Shannon's effectiveness as a teacher, I began to set goals for myself. By the end of the school year, my reading level increased 2.5 years, which meant that I was reading on a seventh grade level in the fifth grade.

Mrs. Shannon's effective style of teaching sparked my interest in wanting to become a teacher. I believe I would not be the teacher I am today if it wasn't for Mrs. Shannon's high expectations for her students.

Her Bark Was Worse Than Her Bite
by
Sheri A. Brown

My seventh grade teacher, Ms. C. Mitchell could be characterized by her robust and intimidating size, and her snide rebuttals for difficult students. In as much, she had a reputation that no knowledgeable student wanted to confront. However, it was in her classroom that my views of science were influenced for the better.

Ms. Mitchell motivated us toward a standard of excellence in our daily work, group work, and project presentations. She would not accept poorly written or "raggedy" work. She would rather give a failing grade than accept unkempt work. But, she would always give you credit for effort even if most of your answers were incorrect. During group work, Ms. Mitchell always reminded us of the importance of teamwork and how our work was a reflection on all of us. This influenced us to be accountable for one another, as well as the desire to please her with almost perfect assignments.

When given a science project, the pressure was high to achieve the expectations that she set in the guidelines. I can remember worrying all night about my project on the solar system. I wanted to make sure that the planet Saturn had the right number of rings around it and the right number of moons. The Earth had to be colored perfectly. I checked the distance between each planet to ensure their visual accuracy. My mother repeatedly tried to assure me that everything was good and that I would receive a good grade, but I was not satisfied. Moreover, the next day was filled with nervousness as I awaited Ms. Mitchell's fifth period class to arrive. I knew that I would have to present my project in front of the class; in front of Ms. Mitchell. When my name was called, I took a deep breath and set up my project. I presented the project. Ms. Mitchell was pleased and she verbally praised my work in front of the class.

Ms. Mitchell required us to put forth an honest effort in our work. Her high expectations for us carried over to other classes and throughout junior high and high school. We later learned that her "bark was worse than her bite." After leaving her class, she befriended me and others. She watched and followed our progress until her retirement.

She Has Always Had My Back
by
Michael L. Fannin

Ask yourself what is an effective teacher? According to Webster's Dictionary, effective is defined as having an intended or expected effect or producing a strong impression or response. I feel that an effective teacher is anyone who motivates, inspires, and encourages someone to go to the next level of learning. They will take any measures that are necessary.

No disrespect to any of my teachers that I've had along the way, but there is no one that can compare to my mother being my teacher. First and foremost, learning starts at home. I think that's what a lot of parents misconstrued about teachers and school. Some parents tend to think that school is the only place where their children should learn. Some parents are not concerned about their children's future. I think that anybody who lets a child go outside to play before attempting to ask that child about any type of homework or just a simple question like, "How was your day at school?" is not a concerned parent. I think that parents should be involved in their child's school any way they can. I think it should be mandatory for parents to come to PTO meetings, and to attend parent-teacher conferences. All-in-all, parents should be more involved.

My mother was the total opposite of the parent that I talked about in the previous paragraph. I think that my mother stayed at the school more than I did. My mother knew my teachers and my teachers knew my mother. My mother was the type of parent who would pop up at the school with no invitation. I never knew when she was coming, so I always had to be on my best behavior at all times.

I give my mother all the praise for motivating me to become a teacher. It didn't dawn on me until later the reasons why she made me stay in the house until I completed all of my work, including the work that she had for me as well. She motivated me in ways that no words could explain. My mother instilled in my brothers and me that being smart was our best ticket to success. Also, she told us that being smart was cool no matter what other students said.

No matter what sport we played, my mother always reminded us that we wouldn't be able to play sports our entire lives. So with that being said, that motivated me to become a great student as well as a great person. She constantly reminded me of people who relied on athletics rather than their education for their claim to riches. Some athletes tend to get hurt or get into some trouble and lose their opportunity to the next level and of course they have nothing else to fall back on but the streets.

I think that my mother fits into more than one of the 12 characteristics of being a good teacher. My mother is encouraging, motivational, inspiring, loving, caring, and most important, she's my mother! So I know she has always had my back and will continue to have my back.

No Contractions
by
Starrah Galloway Huffman

Professional, knowledgeable, and pleasant was Mrs. Julia Scott, my eighth grade English teacher at Eastside Middle School. She was a very attractive woman whose presence commanded attention and respect from everyone with whom she came in contact. She modeled the standard use of the English language at all times, which is what she expected of all her students. For example, we did not use contractions in her class. We said, 'did not' instead of 'didn't.'

Since Mrs. Scott was the eighth grade English teacher, she was also the head of the school's drama club. This organization would perform an annual spring drama for the student body. Mrs. Scott enlisted me to perform the lead part in the drama. Now, I would never say that I am a shy person, but public speaking of any form terrifies me. However, when she told me that I would do the lead part, I had no choice but to oblige her. At the same time, Mrs. Scott had a way of asking you to do something while telling you that you were going to do it.

We practiced and practiced, and rehearsals went well. However, as the production date drew near, fear began to set in, and I wanted to back out. So, I went to Mrs. Scott and explained my fears and apprehensions. I was really there to tell her all of the reasons I could not do the part and to tell her to find someone else.

After I finished, she explained to me all the reasons why I was the perfect person for the part. That was a crucial point in my adolescent life. Growing up, I did not have many people telling me what I could do. That does not mean that I was not encouraged as a youth, but not many people were there to tell me that I could do something like this. Mrs. Scott was the person to do it.

Thus, the production went well, and I experienced a newfound self-confidence. Never before had I felt that way, and I attribute that to Mrs. Scott, whose high expectations enabled me to set aside my fears and apprehensions in order to accomplish the never before, at least for me.

Now, I am an eighth grade English teacher communicating those same high expectations and encouragement to my students. After they tell me what they cannot do, I in turn explain to them every reason why they can.

E. F. Hutton
by
Edward Simms III

I can remember when I first started junior high, there was this history teacher named Mrs. Landry. She taught Louisiana History. She was an elderly white lady whom we (the students) thought was cock-eyed. She drove an old Ford car and never really smiled at anyone.

I had maintained a 3.0 average and made the football team, and as I walked into class, who did I see—Mrs. Landry. I was nervous. She reminded me of E.

F. Hutton. When she talked, everybody listened. I made it a point for her not to know who I was. I studied hard and even though I was used to being a class clown, not in her class.

After the first nine weeks report came, I got a 'C' in her class and I was furious. She told me, "That is what you earned, and that is what I gave you." So I didn't let that stop me. I had a talk with her one morning. The talk we had inspired me greatly. After that I made straight 'A's.

Once I got to know her, I didn't look at her as Mrs. Landry the mean ole lady, but a human being who struggles with everyday life just like my mother and grandmother. I took a strong liking to her and always did my best to stand out. I would be embarrassed if another teacher told Mrs. Landry anything negative about me. If anything, what she taught me was much greater than Louisiana Studies. She taught me a life lesson. I looked at Mrs. Landry as if she were my own grandmother. She showed me that all white people were not racist. That no matter how young or old, all people need to be treated with respect and love.

Our relationship went deeper than the four walls in the classroom. As I moved on to high school, she kept an eye on me. She expected nothing less than the best from me.

When I graduated and came to Alabama State University to play football, she attended at least 4 games a year. She would ride with my mom, sister and grandmother to the games. That meant a lot to me. Whenever I go home, I still go visit her.

One thing I will always remember is the time when I went to visit her at school. I gave her a hug and kiss. I overheard one of her student saying, "What's wrong with him!? Why is he hugging her!?" I responded, "If you really knew her, you would do the same."

Expect the Unexpected
by
Laneshia V. Babers

Looking across the cafeteria, a whole body of fifth graders stood, laughed, cried, and talked as we patiently waited for the calling of our names. It was that time of year again. It was the time to journey off into a new classroom of learning. As I nervously waited for my name, I constantly prayed, "Please Lord, do not let me get Mrs. Kimber for my teacher this year."

I had heard all of the unpleasant, horrifying rumors that came along with being a student in her class. Well, as the crowd of students got fewer and the last teacher, Mrs. Kimber, walked in. I wondered if God had listened to me!? I wondered if he had heard my cry!? I guessed not! When Mrs. A. Kimber called my name, I thought I was going to have the worst fifth grade year ever. Little did I know that Mrs. Kimber's unpleasant and unwelcomed high classroom expectations would teach me how to overcome challenges, difficulties, and frights.

Mrs. Kimber was the most effective teacher that I had. She was the most effective teacher because of the high standards placed on her students. Fifth grade students could not pass her class unless they could learn, memorize, and recite poems, write a speech, and then recite that speech along with all her other demanding coursework.

Learning, memorizing, reciting long poems and speeches were difficult and troublesome problems that I encountered while attending elementary school. I spoke to Mrs. Kimber about my problem. She helped by coming to school early and staying late to practice with me. To overcome my "peer" fright, she advised me to pretend that my audience was an audience of strangers instead of friends. She would ask some of the other teachers and students catching the late bus to stop by her class so they would be an audience for me.

On one occasion, we stayed so late that I missed the late bus. She took me home. On the way home I recall her telling me instead of listening to the radio, we will listen to my reciting of the poems. Poetry and speech became easy for me. It became so easy that I won the fifth and sixth grade poetry contest.

Finally, fifth grade proved to be very challenging in Mrs. Kimber's class. Due to Mrs. Kimber's high standards, hard work, determination, and support, I learned how to overcome my stage fright. I learned poetry is fun! Most importantly, I learned that I should have high expectations and challenge myself to do my very best.

Hola! Como Estas?
by
LaCretia D. Plane

In 1992, I transferred to a predominantly white school called Westview Hills Middle School in Clarendon Hills, Illinois, a suburb about forty-five (45) minutes outside of Chicago, Illinois. I was in the sixth grade and we had to take a beginning exam to see what classes we could take; for example, beginning, average, or advanced classes. I could take advanced courses that allowed me to select a foreign language. I wanted to learn Spanish.

Ms. Jacob was the Spanish teacher and talking with the older children, they said she was very hard and never gave an 'A' as long as she had taught there. That discouraged me some, but I really wanted to take this class. The first day in class Ms. Jacob greeted us, "Hola! Como estas?" We all looked around confused and afraid.

We wondered how she could begin the class with Spanish on our first day. Ms. Jacob explained everything that she expected from us and she explained what we could expect from her.

Her expectations were very high. It seemed to receive an 'A' you would have to donate all your time to learning Spanish. In class, I felt that Ms. Jacob constantly picked on me because she always asked me the hard questions. As the course went on, I was not doing so well and I decided to go have a talk with

Ms. Jacob. When I talked to Ms. Jacob, she explained that I was doing well in her class. I just needed to focus a little more and she explained the reason she asked me the harder questions was to challenge me. Ms. Jacob accomplished her task. I received an 'A' out of her class and I took four more years of Spanish. To this day, whenever I feel I am not giving my all in a class, I think about my talk with Ms. Jacob and how disappointed she would be in me knowing I did not live up to my full potential.

The Boss
by
Frederick Lloyd

The most inspirational teacher in my educational career was Mr. Charles Hall (the Boss). He was the kind of teacher who was not afraid to speak his mind. He told you in no uncertain terms if what you were doing was acceptable or unacceptable. Mr. Hall was my building-trades teacher. He was a very talented man who bricked houses in his free time. He had a reputation of being a tough guy who would go the extra mile for his students. During some classes, he would stop and talk to us about life in general. One quote I remember most of all was, "Son, whatever you do you be the best at it, no matter if you are a garbage man or a street cleaner. You be the best garbage man—the best street cleaner that you can be."

I catch myself remembering the things that he said back then. His words were powerful and mesmerizing to me. Still today, I use his words to help me persevere during the hard times. He has become ill with cancer and is not doing so well. When I visit my friends in Brookhaven, Mississippi, we go on and on about how much Boss' words have helped us become the people we are. If I could touch just one student like Boss touched me, I would consider my career as an educator a success.

The Academic Leader
by
Crystal Green

Twelfth grade was a breeze for me at Stone Mountain High School in Stone Mountain, Georgia. The school is in the Dekalb County School District. I only had five classes, which included Work Study, where I worked at DEK Security. I was a secretary. When I think about my most effective teacher, only one name pops up in my head, Mr. Ralph Simpson, the assistant principal. Although he was not my in-class teacher, there is no teacher that I ever had who had a greater effect on my life. He made everything in the school run smooth and he was very professional at it.

Mr. Simpson was the type of leader that I would want my own children to be guided by. I feel that he was my most effective teacher because he believed in every student who walked in the doors. He gave all students a fair chance at making responsible decisions about life and the education that would one day make or break us. He was always positive and he never brought personal problems to the school. He cared about the students of Stone Mountain and it was a genuine feeling of respect for not only the student but for the entire staff and faculty.

I ran track for the school's team where I made it to the State Championship and he was there to cheer me on as I won the 100-meter. That showed that he was compassionate toward the students. Not only did he come to cheer the track team on but he also came to show support for all the sports and different organization in the school. Mr. Simpson is the prime example of what I want to become as an educator and role model for all of my students.

Mr. Simpson knew when to laugh and smile, but he also knew when to put his foot down and dish out the discipline. He held high expectations for the students. When it was time to graduate, he wrote in my memory book a message that will stick with me forever. He said, "Exceed expectations and use track as a tool to help you make it through college. Once you have that piece of paper no one can take it away." He also told me that failure to prepare is preparing to fail. Mr. Simpson will forever be an inspiration in my life.

My Savior Had Arrived
by
Paula P. Gibbs

I was a junior at Fruitdale High. That year I got the chicken pox, missed cheerleader tryouts, and got a new English teacher. What a way to start the year!

When I first saw him, he looked so young, the youngest teacher I had ever seen. I said he probably just finished college in May and we are his first English class. I thought this class should be pretty easy. My instincts were wrong, because he was far from easy; he came with a vengeance and eager to teach.

Our class had been deprived of being taught by a good English teacher for the previous two years and we knew nothing about writing, predicate nominatives, or literature. We knew nothing and when he started to teach, he immediately saw and knew just how lost we were. I knew by the look in his eyes and the expression on his face that he had high and great expectations. I remember thinking, "He thinks we are a lost cause and so do I. I'm going to fail this class." But little did I know that my savior had arrived.

He took it upon himself to investigate why we had not been taught the English necessities, and when his investigation was complete; he came back with an even stronger momentum. You could see it on his face just how determined he was to teach us what we needed to know in order to graduate the following year.

Our textbook teaches us that for every behavior there is a consequence. I'm certain there were many days he asked himself what behavior did he exhibit to deserve a challenge of such inadequately prepared students. Today, I wonder how many evenings he referred back to his textbooks finding teaching strategies to teach us what we needed to know and how much work it took for him to prepare and readjust his lesson plans to accommodate a class that was less than adequate.

He was losing hair when he came to us and by year-end; he had lost a tremendous amount more. I could see that he was tired but he never gave up on my classmates or me. His strong will and determination to teach did not go unnoticed by us students. He made himself available after school and on weekends. Because he was so determined to teach, I was determined to learn. That was the hardest 'B' that I ever earned in high school and I can say it was well worth the struggle because little did I know that life itself is sometimes a huge struggle. His exams were tough and thought provoking, but always fair and reflected what he had taught. He presented a huge challenge and I accepted it, knowing that I had to succeed simply because he told me that I could do the work. His support, guidance and high expectations will always be remembered and appreciated because of the life lessons that I learned.

He taught me that even when things are tough, you can make it no matter how hard things seem and how tough things are. With guidance, support and encouragement, you can succeed.

There were 14 students to graduate my senior year, and at the end of our year, he left us to pursue other avenues and greener pastures. Four of the fourteen went on to further their education. Two are teachers, one is a nurse, and then there is me. I'll never forget what he taught me about believing hard enough and it can and shall be done.

He was appointed Dean of Education at Mobile University where he has been a faculty member for the past five years. There is nothing greater than having the opportunity to give recognition to someone so humble, yet so great; so today I acknowledge the great impact that he made on me as a student and as a person. I thank him for entering my life and having passed my way.

So, "by the authority of 'me' and on the recommendation of 'me' I hereby confer on Dr. Larry V. Turner the title of 'My Most Effective Teacher in my Lifetime' with all the honors, rights and privileges thereto pertaining on this 26 day of January, 2005."

Creative

Creative - Effective teachers are very resourceful and inventive in how they teach their classes.

Examples:

- ✓ Kissing a pig if the class reaches its academic goals.
- ✓ Wearing a clown suit.
- ✓ Agreeing to participate in a school talent show.
- ✓ Using technology in the classroom.

"Although most people might look for signs of creativity in the appearance of the bulletin boards, student made projects, centers, and displays in the classroom, I feel that the truly creative classroom goes way beyond what can be seen with the eyes. It is a place where bodies and minds actively pursue new knowledge. Having a creative classroom means that the teacher takes risks on a daily basis and encourages his/her students to do the same." (Pann Baltz, 1993 American Teacher Award (ATA) Teacher of the Year as quoted in Creativity in the Classroom: An Exploration - Harvard Graduate School of Education).

The first step in developing the characteristic of creativity is the realization that children learn in many different ways. A creative teacher will incorporate technology, music, dance, drama, art, hands-on activities, and even nature into the lessons. Traditional classroom learning focuses on sitting at a desk, listening to lectures or memorization of facts. For the most part, this has been the norm for K-12 classrooms in America. This stagnant form of learning clearly does not work with today's generation of young people who daily play video games, use cell phones, watch cable T.V., and surf the internet.

A teacher who has the characteristic of creativity will develop a classroom in which all the elements of creativity—space, movement, sound, rhythm, shape, and color are used to provide the most favorable learning environment. A creative teacher will seek to address all learning styles and modalities. A creative teacher will encourage each student to exercise his or her innate curiosity, to experience the joy of discovery learning and the pleasure of learning in a way that he or she learns best.

Over the years, my students have shared how their most memorable teachers expressed creativity. One example is a biology teacher who kept his word and brought a pig to class. He kissed the pig, as he had promised, because the class did well on the unit exam in which he had made his "kissing the pig" challenge.

A principal wore a clown suit and stood on a busy intersection next to the school with a sign stating, "We Reached Our Reading Goal!" because the school reached its Accelerated Reading goal.

A teacher agreed to participate in the school talent show and, in turn, was able to use her performance to teach a lesson on the role that music and dance have played in the American culture. Through activity using technology in the classroom, a teacher found a creative way to successfully teach his lesson by tapping into his students' interest in video games.

The essays presented in this chapter are additional examples of ways in which effective teachers expressed their creativity.

The Jig Dance
by
Latonda Lewis

Highland Gardens Elementary was located in a neighborhood struggling to keep as many Confederate flags hanging from the front porch as possible. In the heart of Montgomery, Alabama, in the 1980s, twenty years outside of the Civil Rights Era, there was still very noticeable racism. Even though Highland Gardens Elementary sat in the midst of a majority white neighborhood, there were just as many African American students as Caucasians enrolled. When I attended Music class, those noticeable differences were diminished immediately. Mrs. Blackwell's style of teaching music was enlightening and transforming in many ways. As I reminisce, I am reminded of many times where Mrs. Blackwell's creativity made her connect easily to all students, regardless of race and color.

I can remember singing songs that made little or no sense to me at the time—songs that told of history, laughter and make believe. Through these songs many lessons were taught, but not by a song alone. Mrs. Blackwell, a short, stout, Caucasian woman, full of life and energy was a constant reminder of the simplicity of life itself. Every piece of enthusiasm that was in her bones, she shared with every student in her presence.

Her way of teaching music was unique and exciting and also very challenging. I am very thankful for the modest creativity that oozed from her to ensure that every song sang, every piece of music taught, was expressed in a way that caught and held my attention!

I remember learning the "jig" dance, as she would call it, by watching her sway from side-to-side as she be-bopped to any fast-paced song. There was a song entitled, *The Robin's Nest*. The song was about how the robin would find things from other animals' habitat to build its nest. She would sing this song while playing her piano, with her robin cap sitting snugly on her head. All of us would get so caught up in her performance that we would soon find ourselves mimicking her every move.

Mrs. Blackwell didn't mind going that extra mile to ensure that the message of a song or a sheet of music was portrayed correctly! I'm not sure how many Mrs. Blackwells are still out there, but to those who fit this persona, I would like to say thank you for using the gift of creativity to teach—to ensure that every child in your class is touched in such a positive way.

He Had This Hippy Thing Going On!
by
Dorethea Coleman

I have always been afraid of math. Adding, subtracting, multiplication and division have always been tolerable, but anything more advanced than that has constantly been a struggle for me. At my high school, the black kids were not encouraged to take higher level math classes. Our guidance counselors never tried to push us to take the algebra, calculus, geometry or trigonometry. All we were told was that we only needed to take basic math and that's what we did. We didn't know we would be handicapped when we got to college (those who were encouraged to attend) and had to take algebra and calculus. That leads me to my favorite math teacher.

I first attended college in the winter of 1986. I did well in all of my classes except for, yep, math. I failed or dropped Finite Math soooo many times that I can't even count them! I took developmental math, but that still did not give me the math skills I needed in order to pass Finite Math—so that I could graduate. Needless to say, after being unable to pass the required math, along will other frustrations, I eventually quit school.

After working many dead end jobs, getting married, and having children, my husband and I decided to go back to school and finish our degrees. It was 17 years later. I had made up my mind that I was not going to let that math class defeat me. I was an adult now, and there was nothing that I couldn't do.

Luckily for me, I enrolled in Mr. William Pilati's math class. Mr. Pilati would become my favorite math teacher. Mr. Pilati was and is very unconventional. He had this hippy thing going on—as if he was stuck in the 1960s—bell bottoms and all, and I really did not know what to expect. Much to my surprise, he was a great math teacher. He taught us Finite Math in a way that you could really understand. I was 35 years old at the time and felt that I could not understand this advanced math when I was 19, how could I understand it now at 35. Not only did I learn Finite Math, I also was able to tutor other students in my class! Mr. Pilati's teaching style and patience enabled me to understand the course and pass it which enabled me to finally graduate with my college degree.

The confidence I gained in his class has also helped me in other areas of my life as well. I no longer allow small things to defeat me. I am now completing my master's degree—something I never dreamed I would be able to do. I give the credit to God and Mr. Pilati.

Traveling the World Without Leaving the Classroom
by
Raye Lambert

I attended first through twelfth grade at one school—Sparta Academy. Therefore, I knew all the teachers and they knew me. But, the most effective teacher I had was my fifth grade teacher. Her name was Mrs. Frierson. She taught Social Studies. The characteristic that I most admired about Mrs. Frierson was her creativity. She was the first and only teacher I ever had that created centers in her classroom. She placed huge pieces of cardboard strategically around the room to create private centers.

Each individual center was decorated precisely to make you feel as if you were in the country we were studying. This type of creativity took great time and effort. We would visit each center and complete the work there before continuing on to the next center. You have to realize that this type of contemporary teaching was not normal at this point in time - I am talking about in 1979.

I remember that I was always excited to go into Mrs. Frierson's classroom because of the creative way in which it was decorated. To me, her mode of teaching was more like a fun play time; however, I learned so much. I was motivated by her unique way of presenting the instructional material.

At the end of each unit of study, Mrs. Frierson would allow us to have a party with food from the country we had studied. She would assign us each a dish to bring and we would all dress like the people of that country. She would play music that was typical of that country during our party.

I am sure it is easy for you to see why I chose Mrs. Frierson as my favorite teacher. It is my goal to be the kind of teacher Mrs. Frierson was. I will strive to create this type of environment in my classroom, so that the students will enjoy the learning experience and be motivated to do their very best. This is what I call an effective teacher!

Learning Through Song
by
LaTasha Davis

There are an abundance of great teachers in this world. Many of them exhibit wonderful qualities that they bestow on their students. I had the pleasure of coming in contact with a teacher named Mr. Tubner. Mr. Tubner was my fourth grade teacher at Oak Street Elementary School in Los Angeles, California. He was a very creative teacher who helped his students learn through music. Being in his class was a joy even though he taught our class for a short time. Mr. Tubner was a compassionate teacher as well as a creative teacher. But my fondest memory was the extraordinary way he taught our lessons.

Being a creative teacher is one of the best characteristics a teacher can possess. Not only does it keep the students' attention, it also stays with the students for a lifetime. As written in the previous paragraph, Mr. Tubner was our teacher for a short time. The teacher who was originally assigned to our class had to leave because of reasons we did not know. The principal told us she was not coming back and Mr. Tubner was going to be our teacher for the remainder of the year. The class was very happy to have him as our teacher.

Mr. Tubner was the music teacher for the school, so every student came in contact with him some time or another. From what I can remember, every student really admired him as a teacher. We were a self-contained class so he taught us all subjects. He incorporated music in every subject he taught to enhance learning.

Being in Mr. Tubner's class was a thrill. We learned the rules for different math objectives through song. Our class also sang the multiplication facts as we used our desks as a drum. A lot of the skills he taught are still with me to this day.

Creativity while teaching can benefit the student and the teacher. Possessing one or more of the characteristics of an effective teacher should be a goal for all teachers. Mr. Tubner possessed these characteristics and he was a very effective teacher. Not only was he an effective teacher, he was also loved and admired for his goodness.

The Golf Game
by
Stan Milton

During my twelve years of public education, I had many wonderful, caring, and intelligent teachers. The most effective teacher that I had during that time was Charles Insinga. He was the first male teacher that I ever had. I feel that some of the reason that I became a teacher is because of him. When I was a student of Mr. Insinga's, he was a sixth grade teacher during the 1989-1990 school year.

Mr. Insinga taught my class math, science, and social studies. I believe that he was an effective teacher because of the creativity of his motivational strategies. He found several ways for us to review for a test. We had the old-fashioned game of calling out questions and students raising their hands to answer them. He also had a review activity called "the golf game." The way this game worked was that the class was divided up into two teams. Sometimes it was boys versus girls, Alabama versus Auburn, etc... The first person from each team came up to the front of the room attempting to hit their golf ball closer to the wall than their opponent. The person that hit the ball the closest to the wall got the right to answer the question first. If this person got it right, their team got a point.

The team with the most points at the end of the game would get a prize, along with the bragging rights until the next time we played. Mr. Insinga would also let us listen to the Atlanta Braves baseball game while we were finishing up our class work. This was a HUGE deal to me! These are just two of the examples of creativity that Mr. Insinga used to inspire us to learn our material. I have patterned many of Charles Insinga's motivational strategies in my own classroom. I would have to say that creativity was Mr. Insinga's greatest characteristic.

The Frog Lady
by
Jimishi J. Lewis-Smith

Thinking back, I can truly remember my fifth grade social studies teacher, Mrs. Hollen. She was a very energetic and creative teacher. She was married with twin girls and she loved any item that dealt with frogs. We called her "Frog Lady" from time to time and she would refer to herself as a frog lover and proud of it.

Mrs. Hollen did not follow the normal social studies textbook method of teaching social studies that many of my previous educators utilized. Compared to any other social studies class that I had in elementary school, I remember Mrs. Hollen's class the most. She involved art activities in her units, and it was always something different. She always participated in school wide activities and dressed up in school colors and for holidays as well. I remember her being very pleasant and humble. All the students respected her because she would not teach above our level of learning and she spoke to us and not at us. Also, if she assigned certain activities that required additional materials, she would always provide her personal items or she would make sure the materials could be found around our home.

In addition to her being such a creative teacher, she was sincere. It is so rare for teachers to have a personal connection with their students as she did. I can remember when we had to complete a report on a historical icon that had a very influential impact on our country. The assignment was to complete a report, do an oral presentation to the class, and provide a visual aid. She gave us this assignment and she actually provided other examples, to include giving a report herself. She actually told me that she wanted to keep my project, which was a wood stained drawing of Harriet Tubman to present to her future classes.

To this day, she still shows my project as an example. I know because she taught my younger brother and he told me about his assignment and the examples she showed his class. I still see her from time to time. She remembers my name and we talk about that assignment. She is still concerned and wants to know how I am doing.

The Smurfs
by
Marteen Streeter

I can reflect back on my fourth grade teacher at C. L. Salter Elementary School, Mrs. Ledbetter. The most effective characteristic that she displayed was creativity. I can still remember the first day of school. The room was decorated with all types of cartoon characters. Our desks were grouped together and each group was individually named after a cartoon character. My group was called the Smurfs. I can remember when Mrs. Ledbetter would call for us to line up for the restroom, lunchroom, and library according to our cartoon characters. She would call, "The Smurfs line up first." I thought that this was the most creative approach of managing our class.

As I reflect back on the lessons that Mrs. Ledbetter taught, I can remember everything being hands-on and we always used different types of manipulatives. For example, one lesson that I can remember was algebraic equations. Her objective was to help students identify how to add and subtract integers. While doing so, she allowed us to dress up as chickens and cows. The chickens were the negatives and the cows were the positives. We made the costumes out of construction paper, newspaper, glue, and string. After the uniforms were created, she explained what negative and positive numbers were by using a number line outlined in our textbook. Then she allowed us, in our uniforms, to act out algebraic equations while actively learning to add and subtract integers. I thought this was very cool and creative, and today I still remember when I subtract and add integers. I always remember, a chicken minus a cow, equals a chicken.

Another example of Mrs. Ledbetter's outstanding creativity was during Christmas time. Mrs. Ledbetter allowed us to create our own holiday stockings using glitter glue. I thought this was the most creative thing that could have happened in our school because it was Mrs. Ledbetter's idea, and because no other class in the school had this idea.

As I reflect back on this specific teacher, I tend to have a creative side. I am constantly engaging my students with creative activities. I have learned that an effective teacher can be creative and teach a student anything that there is to learn. I really do appreciate Mrs. Ledbetter's unique sense of creativity because I have learned from her how to promote academic achievement and interest in each lesson that I teach by just simply being creative.

The Egg Project
by
Melanie Daffin

My childhood was filled with many wonderful memories. Everything from birthday parties to playing on the beach on a hot summer day. Throughout my marvelous years, I've had lots of teachers and mentors that I remember fondly.

I've had some fairly amazing and inspiring teachers during my years of formal schooling. The best were committed and connected to me not only as a student, but as a human being. They expressed a heartfelt concern and respect for me that transcended any subject matter that they were teaching. They supported my search for meaning and purpose that was above and beyond the curriculum offered in the classroom. However, when I'm asked which one of my teachers I remember the most or which one changed my life, one stands out in my mind. Her name is Mrs. Miller.

Mrs. Miller was a bright and beautiful person with many things going for her. She was a great English teacher for sophomores in high school and a wonderful teacher for Sociology and Psychology for juniors and seniors in high school. I had her for both subjects, but her Sociology and Psychology class had the most impact on me. She taught her students the importance of being themselves. Throughout all of her lectures about Freud and other psychologists, she taught us many different ideas and theories that we may or may not have agreed on. She never once made us think that any one theory was better than the other one and she never made us choose one to believe in. She just gave us all the facts and left us to decide which ones we agreed with.

The main reason Mrs. Miller influenced me was because she made everything fun and exciting. For every new concept or idea that she taught us, she had examples. For instance, when she was teaching us about disabilities, she provided class activities to help us to experience what it would be like to have that disability. I had to pretend that I was deaf for a day by wearing earplugs. Another student acted blind by wearing a blindfold during the class. Through real life situations, we learned a lot about ourselves and about how to treat others.

Another example of her creativity was the egg project. She gave us real life scenarios and handed us all eggs. The eggs represented our kids. We had to carry these eggs around everywhere that we went, even to basketball games. If one broke, we had to pay money for hospital bills and possibly a funeral. At the same time, Mrs. Miller gave us a budget that we had to live on. We had to figure out our monthly expenses. Let me tell you, it was an important lesson for all of us. Especially when some people were teenage mothers and were expected to live on $15,000 a year.

I really loved Mrs. Miller. All of her students did. She respected her students and her students respected her. Every time I think of her, my last memory of her pops into my head. Right after graduation, a few of my close friends and I went to say goodbye to her. It was very difficult and challenging because we knew that it was all going to change from that point on. She told us that the best friends that you'll ever have we'll meet in college. Of course, we didn't want to believe that. I knew then that it was only the beginning and we were all going to grow from there. She taught us to be strong.

Mrs. Miller was a lot of things. She was intelligent, funny, caring, and most of all understanding. She understood what it was like to be an adolescent and didn't treat us like we were babies. Of course, if we were good, she gave us suckers from time-to-time!

Giving Back What She Gave To Me
by
Thaddeus Thompson

Children look at their teachers as being heroes. I will never forget that special teacher who helped me decide my career. This special person was Ms. Beverly Stewart, self-contained, third grade teacher, at Lewis Adams Elementary School in Tuskegee, Alabama. She must have had the biggest heart ever. There was never a dull moment in our classroom. The positive atmosphere in the classroom kept a smile on everyone's face. But, that was not the characteristic that made her so great. It was indeed her creativity.

Some of the things she did to motivate the students were unbelievable. She always allowed her students to play a part in decorating the class for the holidays. Ms. Stewart made certain there was something to look forward to each day in our class. For example, she had really nice prizes for those students who performed well during the week. Prizes consisted of trips, parties, and neat little gifts. Every other week she would take a select few students to the movies or skating, or out to eat. She would even invite our parents to come along. It was a wonderful feeling. It made everyone try extra hard, because they wanted to go. She made up activities that helped low achievers succeed. This gave everyone the opportunity to attend the festivities. There was no one in the class who thought they could not succeed. Her methods of teaching were so creative. The excitement in the classroom was like no other. We did a lot of role playing. Students who did not like to talk that much really started to open up in our class. We all competed to be a character. She even had guest to come to the room and speak to us. Some of them were her former students who had succeeded. That was very motivating for us—to see someone she had taught come back and tell us how she had made such a great impact on their lives.

Ms. Lewis is still teaching today. Whenever I get a chance, I talk to her to get encouragement and creative ideas for teaching my class. Her creativity made me want to become a teacher so that I could give back what she gave to me.

More Than Just Worksheets
by
Ashley McCrary

Throughout the years teachers have come and gone, but not many of them stood out in my memory except for one. The teacher that stood out and helped me the most in my academic career was my fourth grade teacher, Ms. Henry. She taught at Bethune Elementary in College Park, Georgia.

She was also very creative. She found new and exciting ways to help us understand our work. I remember when we studied Black History Month, she invited people whose great grandparents were slaves, or whose parents or grandparents were activists involved in the Civil Rights Movement, to come speak to our class. I thought it was so cool! I told all my family members and friends how I had met people who had something to do with Black History.

Now that I think back, her teaching style was so hands-on. I can barely remember just sitting behind my desk and just doing worksheets. We always moved around and explored. Ms. Henry taught us to inquire, ask questions, be adventurous, and find the best solutions.

Fair

Fair – Effective teachers are just in how they treat students and in their grading.

- ✓ They allow all students equal opportunities and privileges.
- ✓ They clarify requirements for the class.
- ✓ They recognize that "Fair" doesn't necessarily mean treating everyone the same, but giving every student what he or she needs in order to be successful.
- ✓ They understand that all students don't learn in the same way and at the same rate.

Children are more concerned about how you treat them than about how you teach them. If children know that you care about them and you will treat them fairly, they will learn and behave properly to please you.

"Recognizing our own preferences and biases is the first step to being fair to our students" (Paul, 2002 p.l). As a teacher, you must look closely at your own feelings toward individual children. Recognize that you bring to the classroom certain attitudes and opinions about different types of children from different backgrounds. Children can sense if they are not liked or if you have "favorites."

An effective teacher will do everything within her or his power to give the appearance of fairness. This includes making sure you equally call on boys and girls and children of different racial groups to answer questions, to be group leaders, and class helpers. You can do this by keeping a checklist.

Regardless of the grade-level or the assignment, students should be given specific guidelines for each assignment, how they will be evaluated, and how successful they were on the assignment once completed. Effective teachers have a classroom environment where students feel comfortable asking questions about class assignments and their grades on assignments.

You must also understand that fair doesn't mean treating all children the same. It is important to remember that children's situations are different, so you must be just in the way you treat their individual situations. You would not expect a child with a problem learning a concept or a child with a learning disability to learn the information at the same rate and speed as other children in your classroom. You must be willing to work with these children one-on-one. Fair means giving each child the tools she or he needs in order to be successful. "Being fair reflects your character, which is the kind of person you are" (Salzmann, 2003 p.3). The following essays share stories of teachers who mastered the characteristic of being fair.

A Lesson In Fairness
by
Curtis Moorer

When I was in the fifth grade, I had an effective teacher named Mrs. Smith. She influenced me to do the right things in life. Mrs. Smith touched many lives during her 25 years of teaching. It seemed to me that she always had a fair personality. I can't remember a time that Mrs. Smith treated anyone in a matter that was unnecessary or unfair. Sex, religion, age, and background were never a factor in her class. If you were causing a disturbance during instructional time, she would have handled the situation according to the child's action.

She rarely involved the parents unless there was no improvement in a child's behavior. Her grading method was another reason why I think Mrs. Smith was fair. If a student failed an exam, she would grade the student on an area that would improve that previous grade. At times, I felt like she was unfair, but I later realized that she was only displaying what was best for the students.

Mrs. Smith spent many days after school tutoring students who were not meeting the requirements in the fifth grade. She was chairperson over the fifth grade department. I later understood some of the methods she used during my experience in her class and I incorporated them in my class. Throughout my many years of education, I never had another teacher quite like her. I sometimes reflect on the times that I had in her class. When I go home to visit, I stop by her house sometimes to let her know how things are going in my life, and how my teaching experience is going.

Three Qualities of My Favorite Teacher
by
Loressa Holman

In today's society, educators are important role models in our students' lives. An effective teacher teaches for their students' best interest and understanding in each subject areas.

My favorite teacher was named Ms. Cindy. She taught third grade at my school. The school was St. Malachy Catholic School of Chicago, Illinois. The main three important qualities Ms. Cindy had were: fairness, compassion, and high expectations.

The first quality Ms. Cindy showed was fairness by allowing all her students equal opportunities and privileges in the classroom. She made all of her students feel special and important in class.

The second quality Ms. Cindy demonstrated was compassion by caring for her students in class and caring about what was going on in our homes. Ms. Cindy would even show up on Saturday mornings to tutor her struggling students.

The third quality Ms. Cindy showed was high expectations. By setting academic standards in her class, she built confidence and motivation. She believed in her students. Effective teachers are important role models in students' lives.

The Light Bulb Effect
by
Aundria Sewell

An effective teacher is one who holds many characteristics. This type of teacher reaches his/her students in a positive way. In thinking back to my primary years (K-3) in school, I would say that I was lucky enough to have at least two effective teachers and maybe three. However, the teacher that I remember most clearly in the actions he took in making sure his students were actually learning and that he was making a difference was Mr. Smith.

Mr. Smith taught first grade at Raymond Avenue Elementary in Los Angeles, California. Mr. Smith's classroom consisted of half English-speaking students and half Spanish-speaking students. This wasn't a hard situation to contend with because Mr. Smith spoke Spanish fluently. He possessed a personal touch in dealing with a classroom full of first graders. In fact, no matter if you spoke English or Spanish, he made you feel important and he made you feel as though he knew exactly what you needed to get that "light bulb effect." Mr. Smith was fair, creative and positive as well.

I remember one incident where Mr. Smith decided to have a sort of spelling bee in the classroom. The words included were English as well as Spanish. One way that he made the game fair was the English speaking students had to spell the English words. But, if you could spell the word in both English and Spanish, you would get some type of bonus points. In the end, both English and

Spanish speaking students learned the meaning and spelling of a number of words in both languages. I think Mr. Smith was an effective teacher and one that made a difference in a lot of young children's lives—myself included.

Giving So Much of Himself
by
Predencia Dickerson

Ronald Haygood III taught ninth grade English. He was one of the best teachers Booker T. Washington High School ever had. Mr. Haygood was the type of teacher who made you want to learn. Every week he would give us a different proverb and we would have to say it everyday. They were proverbs to get his students motivated. After each test, he would take out to dinner the top three students with the highest test scores. He gave a lot of work but it was all useful.

Students could talk to Mr. Haygood about anything. He was a very understanding and caring person. If a student missed class who did not usually miss class, he would call their parents to make sure that they were all right. He would share his personal experiences with the class just to let us know that he understood whatever was going on.

Mr. Haygood was at every PTA meeting to let parents know how their child was doing in his class. He loved to brag on his students. He was very proud of us. He said I was one of his favorites. If a parent could not make it to a PTA meeting, he would call and give the parent an update on their child. Mr. Haygood emphasized repeatedly that students and/or parents could call him at anytime.

He was fair with each one of his students. Whenever they needed help, they could always go to him. He was the type of teacher who would laugh and joke with students as long as we had finished our work first. He would put stickers on our papers with encouraging and praising words.

Mr. Ronald Haygood III was the best teacher I ever had. He made sure that his students knew that he cared about them and their future. Mr. Haygood is the only teacher that I have ever had that gave that much of himself. He is a great teacher and a great mentor.

Caught Cheating
by
Alicia D. Cheatham

The teacher that I have selected is my fourth grade teacher, Mrs. Wanda Pickens. She taught at Colbert Heights Elementary. Mrs. Pickens taught fourth grade in a restricted classroom. Therefore, she taught all subjects. She was an effective teacher because she was fair. An example was one incident when I was absent from school for almost a week. Actually, Mrs. Pickens and I were both absent from school because there was a virus going around and both of us caught it. The two of us were absent from Wednesday through Friday.

On Monday, we both returned and she noticed that I had not taken my spelling test. Therefore, she gave me and my neighbor, Stephanie, the test. I told Stephanie that I didn't know my spelling words because I had missed so many days of school the prior week. She told me not to worry about it and I could copy off her paper. I had never done this so I was really nervous about cheating. She told me to lean over enough to see what she was writing. This was not a good idea because Mrs. Pickens was at her desk calling the words out to us.

When Mrs. Pickens noticed what I was doing, she came and got my paper and wrote a big zero on my paper. I was so devastated!! I never knew how it felt to cheat. So I began to cry. Mrs. Pickens called me to her desk and asked me why I was copying off Stephanie's paper. I told her that I had been absent three days last week and I did not know the words. She asked me, "Did Stephanie know you were copying off of her?" Not wanting to get Stephanie in trouble, I said, in a teary voice, "Nooo!"

Mrs. Pickens gave me a speech on how cheating was wrong and gave me a chance to take the test the following Friday. When Friday came I was ready for the test and I made a 100. Mrs. Pickens handed my paper back and said that was the kind of work she expected of me and nothing less.

That was my first and last encounter with cheating and a feeling that I never want to feel again. Mrs. Pickens displayed the characteristic of being fair because she did not have to give me another chance, but she did. Mrs. Pickens knew my personality and this was not a particular behavior of mine. I am thankful to have had a teacher who not only taught, but also displayed good moral judgment.

Personal Touch

Personal Touch – Effective teachers are approachable.

✓ They connect with students in a personal way.

✓ They share personal experiences with the class.

✓ They take a personal interest in the students and find out as much as possible about them.

✓ They visit the students' world (neighborhoods, homes, sit with them in cafeteria, etc.).

✓ They come to sporting and other events outside normal school hours.

"If we respect and care about each of the children and treat each of them as special, valuable individuals, they are much more likely to have a positive attitude toward our lessons and respect and care about us. We should make it our business to get to know every student's name, what they're interested in, get to know their families, and much more. We should know just as much about the badly behaved children as the well behaved children, and just as much about the quiet children as the noisy ones, and still treat them all the same. If we can find it in us to respect and love each of the children, there's a very good chance they will respect and love us in return." (David Paul – Principal of David English House in Hiroshima, Japan).

This chapter is one where students had a lot to say about teachers they encountered who had the characteristic of *Personal Touch*. The essays you read in this chapter confirm the fact that children want a teacher they can relate to and who can relate to them.

Students learn best in an interactive, open environment. They want a teacher who truly cares about them. It is vital that teachers value their students as human beings and respect their feelings. A personal touch requires the teacher to take a personal interest in each student.

You can begin establishing a personal touch with your children on the very first day of class by introducing yourself and telling your class something about yourself. You can then allow the students to do the same.

You should learn each of your students' names as soon as possible and address them by their name. There is nothing more endearing to us then being called by our name.

Visit students' homes, or at least, drive through the neighborhoods. Driving through the neighborhoods will give you a feel of the community environment where your children live. Going to sporting events, concerts, recitals, or plays that your children are involved in are all excellent ways of creating a *Personal Touch* with your students. Get to know the parents of your students..

In dealing with students, Memphis City School Psychologist, Annette Woods, Ed.S., states, "It is all about building relationships. I encourage teachers to get to know their students and learn as much as they can about their families, their backgrounds, and their different learning styles."

As an effective teacher, your goal is to develop relationship skills and relate effectively with diverse student families and cultures (Sadkler, 2005).

As you will see from the following heart warming true stories about teachers who had a personal touch, developing a caring relationship with students is vital not only to their academic success, but most importantly—to their emotional well being.

She Knew Exactly How I Felt
by
Allison Smith

During my fifth grade year at Southside Middle School in Tallassee, Alabama, my family experienced a life changing tragedy. My mother was diagnosed with breast cancer. Not only were we faced with this problem, but I fell and broke my leg two weeks later. I was on crutches for twelve weeks.

Because my mother was in and out of the hospital so much and my dad staying with her, my brother and I were going back and forth between home and my aunt's house. Not only were we upset about our mom, but we now had to share a room with three other children. We were not use to this type of living arrangement and we had a hard time adjusting. My mom stayed sick all the time because of the chemo that she was taking. It was very hard for an eleven year old to sit and watch her mother brush out her hair and not understand why. My brother and I being so young really did not understand what was going on or how to handle the situation.

It was extremely hard for one person, being my aunt, to make sure that five children did homework, ate supper, took baths, and got in the bed at a decent time. She did the best that she could, but it just was not enough. With all the changes that were taking place in my life, my school performance decreased drastically.

My social studies teacher, Mrs. Ruthanne McCaig, noticed the change in my school work and acted upon it immediately. The best characteristic that she displayed was having the best personal touch possible. She sat me down one day after school and explained how she went through the exact same thing when she was a little girl that I was going through at the present time. She knew exactly how I felt and what I was going through. Everyday after that she stayed after school with me and made sure that I completed all of my homework. Because of her, my grades were back to normal and I was able to deal with my mother's situation better.

After sitting down and talking with Mrs. McCaig, I had this feeling that my mom was going to be okay and that I could be a kid again. My mom has been cancer free for 14 years and Mrs. McCaig is the reason that I am a teacher today.

"Run, Kisha! Run!"
by
Kisha Robbins

Throughout my schooling, I have encountered both effective and ineffective teachers. Some were forgettable and others unforgettable. The one that stands out the most would be Ms. Davis.

Ms. Davis was my 6th grade teacher at Powell Elementary in Jackson, Mississippi—it was a self contained class. I can remember it as if it were yesterday; all the stories she would tell the class while she sat on the edge of her desk. There was one particular story I felt she was directing at me. During this period of my life, I always kept a scowl on my face. She told a story about a friend of hers that had been killed in an accident and who also kept a frown on her face. She said that the only time her friend would smile was while she was singing and how pretty she was when she smiled. While she told this story, she was looking directly at me and from that point on I have been cautious of my expression. She didn't fuss like others, she simply told a story.

I also remember going on a field trip and the bus not having enough seats for all the children. Ms. Davis chose me to ride with her. While in the car, we talked about my home life, where I wanted to go to school, and where I wanted to live. I can still remember my answers; Mississippi State and Alaska. She told me that she had once lived in Colorado. I remember wanting to share things in my life with her because she always told us about things in hers.

I remember our statewide field day and competing in the track meet. Ms. Davis convinced me that I could run. I came in second, but I didn't care, Ms. Davis was cheering me on. I can still see her now in her white outfit and that red short curly wig, jumping up and down shouting, "Run, Kisha! Run!" And to top the day off, after the meet, she drove me home.

I felt that Ms. Davis was showing me favoritism, giving me rides, talking about my family and coming to my track meet. But looking back, she just didn't do special things for me but for the entire class. I guess she just had a personal touch that made each one of us feel as if we were her favorite. Thanks Ms. Davis.

Dealing With Death
by
Dennis Lawry

Growing up in a small town in Wisconsin, everyone knew each other. In 1971, the village of Oregon only had around 1,000 residents. Our school, Oregon Middle School, was a combination of our town and two surrounding towns which gave each grade somewhere around 125 students. Our school was divided into four units and I was placed in Unit B with Mrs. Henry as the lead teacher. I had Mrs. Henry for both 5th and 6th grade. She taught English and Reading.

Mrs. Henry was a short woman, barely five feet tall, but she was not afraid of anyone, nor was she intimidated by her taller students. She had many of the characteristics that we associate with an effective teacher. She was positive, believing anyone could attain success, no matter who you were or where you came from. She was fair, giving everyone the opportunity they needed. Mrs. Henry was forgiving and respectful. She would always say "yes sir" when answering one of my many questions.

There was not a doubt that Mrs. Henry had high expectations for all her students. She had grown up in the community and knew what it took to be a good citizen. Mrs. Henry was also compassionate, and her students felt a sense of belonging to the class. Everyone knew her, she had been around for years, and most of us were excited to be in her unit.

I think what I will remember most about Mrs. Henry was her personal touch in the classroom, especially to me, or it seemed to me. Mrs. Henry and I built a solid relationship during my 5th grade year. I was different from most other students in that I was already six feet tall and weighed over 200 pounds. She kept me busy, building my self-esteem, pushing me to succeed, and finding ways I could express myself. It was Mrs. Henry who encouraged me to write; and write, I did—until another teacher in high school burst that balloon.

Mrs. Henry made me feel important. That feeling of confidence helped me over the summer between my 5th and 6th grade years. My grandmother became ill and had a series of strokes and heart attacks in June of that year, succumbing on June 29th. I was devastated. Here was the woman that I lived with the most, gone.

My mother kept me away from most of the illness, so I was shocked when this happened. I had not experienced death before, and I was not handling it very well. I became withdrawn, not wanting to be near anyone, maybe thinking they would die as well.

Mrs. Henry knew my grandmother and came to the visitation and funeral. I was glad she was there, but didn't reach out for help. Over the next couple of weeks, Mrs. Henry kept in touch with my mother, checking on how I was doing. She called me one day and asked me to meet her at school. I went because I liked doing things for her. Mrs. Henry wanted me to clean her bookshelves and rearrange them before the next school year began, or so I thought. We began working on the shelves, all the while she asked me questions, chatting about things, and finally she asked me about my grandmother's death.

I didn't know what to say, but that was fine with her. We talked and worked all afternoon, and when I left, she gave me a book, the title of which I do not remember, but it had poems about death, mostly from the Native American point of view—death as being the rebirth, death as a beautiful end to life.

Mrs. Henry met with me several times over the course of the summer, helping me with my poetry writing, and helping me deal with the pain. I had notebooks full of writings that I did for myself and Mrs. Henry.

Sixth grade began with me still dealing, but not dwelling on death. I got involved in a writing contest, thanks to Mrs. Henry. We had to write a composition about Wisconsin history. About the time October came around, my composition, as well as the five or six others in class that were competing in the state contest, was finally completed. Mrs. Henry sent them off and we returned to normalcy in the classroom—until Halloween night, when Mrs. Henry's son was killed in a car accident. We found out about her son the next morning when we all showed up at school and Mrs. Henry was not there. She was always there, but not this morning. We knew something was wrong. My mother explained to me that night what had happened. I immediately wanted to go to her, to be by her side, to hold her hand, to support her. But I was not allowed.

The next morning at school, I asked classmates to help me raise money to send flowers. We collected what we could and gave the money to the school secretary who promised to buy flowers and get them to Mrs. Henry.

Mrs. Henry had a private service for her son, just family, so none of us got to go. My mother told me that Mrs. Henry was taking it very hard, because he was her only child, and not to be surprised if she did not come back to school. But she did—after the Christmas break.

When she finally came back, I was ready for her. I had my book of poems I had written after my grandmother had passed. I gave her that book and told her that I loved her and she could count on me if she needed someone to lean on. We did have our little talks again, usually after school. I don't know if I helped her, but I sure was going to try to help her like she had done for me.

Mrs. Henry has always been my inspiration to become a teacher, trying to do for others, what she did for me. I got sidetracked along the way, but I finally did become what she had been for me. She passed several years ago, but she is still the inspiration, the guidance, and the role model I will always remember.

I Love You
by
Angela Rembert

The teacher who had the most profound positive effect on my life was my sixth grade teacher, Mrs. Beatrice Marsh at North Birmingham Elementary School. She possessed several characteristics that made her the epitome of an effective classroom teacher. Each morning she would begin her class with a personal experience about her education. She had the ability to create an atmosphere in her classroom that made her students eager to learn.

I often reflect on the words Mrs. Marsh would say to us at the end of each school day, "If nobody has told you I love you today…I do!" Those words made the difference in my attitude and my determination to make the teacher I idolized proud.

Going Into Labor
by
Carla A. Brown

My most effective teacher was my 12th grade teacher, Mrs. Strickland. I called her Mrs. S, since I had a hard time saying words that began with 'str'. She was my yearbook staff teacher. I only had her for one year, but she touched my heart in a very special way.

I became pregnant my senior year in high school, and being only 17, I was scared. She talked to me and told me don't let a child stop me from accomplishing any of my goals. She was by my side 110 percent. She gave me her phone number and told me to call her when I went into labor. My mom called her when I went into labor. She was there two hours after my delivery with many gifts. I never thought she would take the time out to come on her day off from work to see me. On that day, I knew she really cared about me.

Mrs. Strickland is no longer at Highland Home High School. I saw her about two months ago and we exchanged numbers. Now we keep in touch. She gives me feedback on how to be an effective teacher. She told me that she knows I will make an excellent teacher because I love children and I am a people person.

Eating With, "Those People"
by
Carla A. Brown

My most effective teacher was Ms. Mary McDowell, my 12th grade English teacher at A. H. Parker High School in urban Birmingham, Alabama. She was my most effective teacher because she had a personal touch with her students, and always showed us respect.

The event that occurred that made her not only my most effective teacher, but also influenced me personally, occurred during a field trip. She arranged for her Creative Writing class to attend a performance at the Celebrity Dinner Theatre. The performance was at night and we had to have our own transportation. But, if we went, we would get our dinner at a discount. At this performance, we saw *Arsenic and Old Lace*. There must have been a group from a nursing home there on that night because there were several elderly white people there.

We had been seated and was about to order when an old white lady asked Ms. McDowell how she could sit and eat with "those people." We all knew that she was referring to us (black people).

Ms. McDowell's face turned fire red as she sat there for a few seconds with her mouth open. She then turned around and loudly stated, "These people are my students and I eat with them because I choose to. They are an intelligent group of young people and I am happy to be their teacher and also be a part of their lives!"

That event taught me a lot about the ignorance of some people. I knew that racism existed. But I had not personally experienced it. The year was 1983 and the Civil Rights Movement was almost 20 years old. We later found out that Ms. McDowell had participated in the Civil Rights Movement. She told us that she was somewhat taken aback by the comment of the elderly lady, but she was not surprised about the attitudes of some old white people. The fact that Ms. McDowell showed respect for her students and spoke up for us in the face of racism definitely made her my most effective teacher.

Dealing With A Divorce
by
Wyconda Lewis

The teacher that I deemed to be an effective teacher was Mrs. Auburtin. She had many characteristics of an effective teacher. The characteristic that I chose to elaborate on is personal touch. Mrs. Auburtin was a very unique teacher. She took time to learn as much as she could about her students. When I was in elementary school, I didn't understand why she took the time to have conversation with her students. She would always sit with us in the cafeteria and ask how we were doing and what we did over the weekend or over the holidays.

Mrs. Auburtin took this time out to establish a relationship with us because she cared. I remember the time when my days at school were not what they used to be. I was worried because my parents were not getting along at home. Mrs. Auburtin noticed the difference in my personality and knew that something was going on in my life but she didn't know exactly what. She told me that she was going to a picnic on Saturday and invited me to go with her. Mrs. Auburtin told me that she would call and ask my mother if I wanted to go. I told her I would like to attend the picnic with her. When I got home that afternoon, she called my mother and asked would it be okay for me to go to a picnic with her on Saturday. My mother told her that it was okay with her but I had to be back at home no later than 6:00 p.m.

Mrs. Auburtin asked my mother was I sick because my personality was not the same. She told her that I was not as joyful as I used to be. My mother explained to my teacher that she and my father were having problems at home and they were in the process of filing for a divorce.

On Saturday, we had a wonderful time and she explained some things to me about divorce. Mrs. Auburtin informed me that both of my parents loved me the same and if they got a divorce it would not change their love for me. Mrs. Auburtin gave me the reassurance I needed that everything would be alright.

Slackers Beware
by
Benetta Eutsey

When you speak of effective teachers, there is one who comes to mind. Mrs. Carolyn Horn taught 5th grade English at Dannelly Elementary School in the early 70s. At that time, however, I thought Mrs. Horn was one of the sternest teachers alive. But life experiences as a layperson and as an educator have made me realize that she only wanted what was best for her students.

Mrs. Horn held us to the highest of standards and had a very low tolerance for slackers and those who misbehaved. She did have a lighter side though. She could be nice and took a personal interest in our general welfare. She formed bonds with our parents and discussed issues other than those that dealt with us as her students. She went beyond what was required by the local, state, and federal guidelines.

Mrs. Horn was the type of educator and person that really connected with the students in a personal way by sharing some or her personal experiences with us. It didn't stop there. She actually invited us (my brother, a neighbor, and me) to her home on several occasions. I'm talking about a white teacher and a few black children from the projects, during the early 70s. As a nation, and more specifically in Montgomery, Alabama, we were not that far removed from the tumultuous 60s and its racial unrest. In my opinion, her personal interest was uncommon for the times. She let us do little things for her around her home and in return, she gave us pencils, rulers, erasers, peppermint candy, etc. We really thought we were special. Mrs. Horn was definitely a teacher who got to know us on a personal level and that is one of the characteristics that made her an effective teacher.

Decorative Paraffin Soap
by
Tiffany Coen

I had a lot of teachers that I adored. However, there is one that stands out. The teacher that I remember most was Mrs. Pforte from Marianna, Florida. She was my 5th grade teacher. Since I was a new student, not only in her class, but at the school, she made it exceptionally bearable for me. I instantly took to her. She was really funny and I knew that she liked me. She made learning fun. I remember one day for Christmas holidays, we had a craft day. She taught us how to make ornaments from eggs and helped me make decorative paraffin soap gifts. My parents still have some of the ornaments I made.

She made me leader for many group projects and that made me feel special. I think that would make any child feel special, particularly when a child is in a new place with no friends. She makes me want to be like that. Not to pick a "favorite" student, but to make every student feel that they are special. That year, I made 'A-B' honor roll and received the Presidential Fitness/Academic award. I was really proud and so were my parents.

Looking back at it, I think the reason why I did so well was because I felt important. Students do better when they feel like they are important and/or loved. Her eagerness to get to know her students and to form personal relationships with them is something I looked up to. It is something that I will strive to do. I just hope that there will be a student who finds me to be their favorite teacher as I found her to be mine.

Academic Struggles
by
Linda Floyd

Because the profession of teaching is a varied one, there are certain aspects of teaching that are the same at all levels. Through effective teachers, the cultural heritage of a society is passed on to new generations. When I was attending Heigber Elementary School, the most effective teacher was Mrs. Brown—my fourth grade teacher.

Mrs. Brown always had that personal touch. She knew just the right words to say. For example, while I was in her classroom, I had to leave for an hour a day to attend Title I Reading. At the time, reading was my only weak subject. Students in the class would tease me and the other students who had to leave out by saying, "They are going to the slow class." Mrs. Brown immediately said to the students, "That was not a nice thing to say." She shared her personal experience about not being able to comprehend what she read. She went on to explain that just because you're not good in one subject or area doesn't mean that you can't improve. She told us that because reading was one of her weak areas, she became proficient in it by attending remediation classes and turned her reading weakness to her strength.

By having the courage to share with us her own past academic struggles, I realized that Mrs. Brown was a teacher who had the characteristic of effectively teaching to students' needs. Her compassion for learning and teaching in a personal way has made her a role model that has nurtured many generations of students.

The First Day of School
by
Robert Price

My education as a child was very eclectic. I am the eldest of five children. My father was an army officer and my mother an English and Art teacher. Few teachers stood out in my early years of school. I attended three elementary schools in Germany and England, and two junior high schools in Texas and Georgia. It was not until high school that one teacher distinguished himself as not only an effective teacher, but as a mentor and friend. This teacher exemplified all 12 of the traits found in an "Effective Teacher," but he excelled in the "Personal Touch" most of all.

I began high school as not only an entering freshman, but as a new resident of the town. My father served as advisor to the National Guard in Eufaula, Alabama. My first day was like any other first day. It was registering, finding new classes, meeting new teachers, and seeking new friends.

During lunch, I ran into my first snag of the day — I forgot my lunch money! I realized this as the checkout lady asked for my money. When I told her that I forgot my money, I heard a voice behind me. I turned around and there stood a teacher telling her he would pay for my lunch. He told me his name, Mr. Pete Walker, and said, "If you get a chance you should take my history class." I recognized his name, and told him I was in his class later that day.

Mr. Walker befriended me on the very first day of school at a very critical time of the day — lunch! There was no way I would act up in his class.

His class was not a cake walk. He always told us we could do more than we ever thought. He pushed us to want to do better in all things. He coached wrestling, baseball, and sponsored many extracurricular activities so he had my attention outside of school as well. Mr. Walker would discuss career and school choices with us. If we were interested in something he found a way to expose us to it by inviting speakers, taking us on field trips, or obtaining information for us.

Two years later, my junior year in school was clicking along nicely when one day I was riding my motorcycle and I was hit by a car. I spent six days in the hospital and was at home in bed for two weeks before returning to school.

Mr. Walker stopped by the hospital each day with my work from my teachers. Once I was at home, he would bring my work by, and even helped me with my calculus! I didn't even know he knew calculus.

After high school, I joined the Army to be a paratrooper. The day I graduated Airborne School in Fort Benning, Georgia, my parents came and brought Mr. Walker. My parents ran into him at lunch several days before and told him I was about to graduate. Fort Benning is only 35 miles from Eufaula, but it felt like a million miles away. I knew my parents would be there, but Mr. Walker was an unexpected guest, but not a surprise. He was that kind of teacher.

The last time I saw him was at his funeral. I was not surprised at how many former students attended. I could not help but to hope that I develop the same relationship with my students as he did with me.

Sticky Pad
by
Jacquelyn Thomas

I have spent most of my life as a student and have come in contact with many educators. Some were effective and some didn't leave any impression at all. However, as I look over my 19 years of formal education, there is one teacher who stands out in my mind. She was my seventh grade teacher, Mr. Loretta Kiser.

Mrs. Kiser taught 7th grade English at Millbrook Junior High School. She left a lasting impression on my life. It was not because she cared when no one else did, or that she believed in me; No, no, it was because of the simple things—her personal touch. Mrs. Kiser made sure that she took time to greet me each morning. Her warm smile brightened even my darkest days. She also took an interest in me. If I were absent from school, she would call my house and make sure that I was okay. She would even go so far as to write a note on a sticky pad that said "I missed you," when I returned to school.

Once Mrs. Kiser heard that I was going to sing at church. She asked me what church I attended and wished me luck. That Sunday, as I scanned the audience, I noticed a familiar face. Low and behold, it was Mrs. Kiser! I couldn't believe that she had come to hear me sing. It meant the world to me. Lastly, Mrs. Kiser had a mother's touch when it came to discipline. If I got out of line, she would gently, yet firmly, put me in my place. I didn't mind that because I knew she genuinely cared for me. As an educator, I learned a thing or two from Mrs. Kiser. I too try to add a personal touch to my classroom.

Staying After School
by
Ranelle Weathers

My most effective teacher was Mrs. Mayes. Mrs. Mayes was my third grade teacher at Jeffries Elementary School. Mrs. Mayes taught all of my general studies (Math, English, Reading, and Spelling). My science, art, and physical education classes were in other classrooms with other teachers. At the beginning of the school year while in Mrs. Mayes class, it was a struggle. I had problems with reading and spelling. I was in the lower level reading group and hated to read aloud. As far as my spelling went, it was not good at all. It was very poor. I received so many N's (Need Improvement) on my papers as well as my report cards that I just gave up. I would not practice my spelling words or reading unless I was instructed to do so in class. Then one day everything changed.

Mrs. Mayes kept me after school to talk so she could find out what was wrong. She said that she could tell that I was not trying. She offered to help me before or after school if it was okay with my parents. Mrs. Mayes and I worked together two days of the week for the remainder of the school year. My grades started to improve, my spelling improved, my reading improved and most important—my confidence.

Once I moved to the next grade, Mrs. Mayes continued to help me. That is why I believe Mrs. Mayes to be my most effective teacher. I will never forget her, and I will always be thankful. She did not have to do what she did for me.

Thick Pink Eye Glasses
by
Sandra L. Rackley

My third grade teacher was Mrs. Wilson. One characteristic that identifies Mrs. Wilson would be a personal touch. When I was in the third grade, I was very shy about reading out loud in the classroom. I was afraid that my classmates would make fun of the way I read and mispronounced words. Everyday Mrs. Wilson would have her students read from one of the textbooks. She would go down the row and have each student read one or two paragraphs. When she got to me, I would speak very softly and hold my head in the book. She would ask me to hold my head up and speak louder so everyone could understand what was being read.

One day she asked me to stay inside for P.E. so I could help her clean the chalkboard. I did not know that Mrs. Wilson wanted me to stay inside and read to her. She discovered that I could read and had a little problem pronouncing words but nothing that could not be improved.

She also discovered that the reason I was holding my head in the book was because I could not see the print. She sent me to the nurse's station to get my eyes checked. I found out that I needed glasses. Not only was I chunky, but now I had to wear glasses. I went home that day with a letter from the nurse stating I needed glasses, and I needed to see an eye doctor immediately.

One week later, I had a pair of thick pink glasses that I had to wear while reading. I told my teacher that I did not like the glasses and I did not feel pretty in them. Mrs. Wilson told me that the glasses looked nice on me and that beauty comes from within a person (Easy for her to say—she wasn't stuck walking around wearing a thick pair of pink glasses!).

She told me a personal story of how she had to wear braces on her teeth. My teacher told me that she was afraid to talk believing that someone would make fun of her. Mrs. Wilson and I had a connection that made me feel wonderful inside and more confident about reading.

I currently wear contact lenses in order to see and perform many tasks. As a teacher, I make sure that all my students' eyes are examined by the school nurse, and if they need glasses, I make sure they get them.

A Part of Our World
by
Kenyon Berry

When I think back over the teachers who influenced my learning and enhanced my career, I can smile and feel proud. The teacher that highly motivated me to learn was my sixth grade teacher. She was my most effective teacher. I have had several teachers over the course of my career. I guess the questions are, "Why did I reach back to my sixth grade teacher? What made her so special? What did she do to make a lasting impression on me?"

My sixth grade teacher was Mrs. Williamson. She taught me at Brighton Elementary School in Portsmouth, Virginia. I will always remember her because she cared about me. She was sensitive and showed compassion for all her students. Mrs. Williamson added her personal touch to teaching. For example, she would place us in groups and discuss news events. She shared her news events with us and discussed what it meant to her. She also asked us to share our news events and personal challenges with the group. She asked us what the topic meant to us. She encouraged our little minds to think of "What if?", "How come?", "Why not?", and "How can?" Mrs. Williamson made the students feel that they were a part of her world. She was definitely a part of ours.

Mrs. Williamson demonstrated her personal touch in many ways. For example, if I were absent from school, she would contact my family regarding my absenteeism. She would call my house periodically to give my parents a progress report. If I didn't do my homework she would counsel me, not in a threatening and scorning manner but in an understanding and caring way. She explained why I needed to do my assignments. Mrs. Williamson also explained that if I studied, it would help me to be successful in life. She would explain how doing my homework would help me. She told me that I could grow up to be a teacher, lawyer and/or anything I wanted to be. Mrs. Williamson also explained that I could buy a beautiful home and have nice things.

Where Babies Come From
by
Debra Todd

The teacher who has left a mark on my mind is my fifth grade teacher, Mrs. Korran, at Southwood Elementary School in Columbus, Ohio. Mrs. Korran was about six months pregnant when school started that fall. So, for the first half of the school year we ate. We had food from around the world. She encouraged us to bring food that we ate everyday in our homes. I brought roasted vegetables, because I refused to eat meat until I was about 15. Everyone loved the vegetables; and I got my first real boyfriend, Kenny. He said he liked my vegetables and wanted a woman who could cook.

Mrs. Korran was Jewish. Therefore, we had to eat everything Jewish. We had lox, fried potatoes, and bagels and some kind of bread that was flat. Not only did we eat, we learned. We learned about each culture that went along with each food. She gave us the opportunity to know ourselves and others.

After Mrs. Korran had her baby, we had a class discussion about where babies come from and the delivery process. I also remember her husband coming in one day with the baby. They let us observe what babies do, how you are supposed to hold them, and what to do if they are choking or have a fever.

This was the best school year of my life. I learned so much from Mrs. Korran. I had no idea what road life would take me down, but I knew I was prepared for whatever came my way.

A California Girl
by
Tiffany R. Anderson

During my senior year at Lincoln High in San Diego, California, I had the pleasure of meeting Mrs. Janet B. Singleton. She was a short, loud, and enthusiastic woman who meant business. Mrs. Singleton was the type of teacher you either loved or hated; there was no in between. Her mouth was quick, mind witty, and heart full. She possessed the personality needed to be a positive role model for inner-city youth.

I consider Mrs. Singleton to be an effective teacher because she always placed a personal touch to education. One particular event comes to mind when I recall her superior teaching ability. Mrs. Singleton believed that every student could attend college if they put their mind to it. She often talked about the importance and excitement in supporting historically black institutions. In December 1999, Mrs. Singleton wanted to take me on a tour of HBCU's (Historical Black Colleges and Universities) on the East Coast. She asked my mother if I could fly with her over the Christmas holiday for some campus tours. She assured my family that my room and board would be covered. She also would provide a full-length leather coat, gloves, and a scarf, since an original California girl like me would not have the proper attire for a real winter. After confirming our travel plans and trip details, we were off to Norfolk, Virginia.

In Virginia, I toured the campus of Hampton University and Norfolk University. During our 2-week vacation, Mrs. Singleton treated me like her own child. She was comforting, respectful, and honest. I enjoyed every minute of that experience. She gracefully crossed the line placed between teacher and friend, while expressing her personality and professionalism.

As I look back on Mrs. Singleton's ability to teach from the heart, I can honestly say she placed a personal touch on my life. To this day, I believe my trip to Norfolk, Virginia, played a major factor on my professional career choice—simply because a short, loud, and opinionated teacher took a chance and provided a little hands-on experience. Mrs. Singleton is a perfect example of an effective teacher.

The Most Inspiring Teacher of My Lifetime
by
Jamille Dorsey

Throughout my younger years, I have encountered a variety of teachers and their unique teaching styles. Of all the teachers who have taught me, there was one unique teacher who stood out. Mrs. Isabella was my fifth grade teacher who taught at Kendrick Middle School located in Jonesboro, Georgia. She made a tremendous impact on my life. Mrs. Isabella exhibited all of the characteristics of what an effective teacher should possess. She taught the entire recommended subject areas required in the school curriculum. Mrs. Isabella always went the extra mile for her students. She always had hands-on materials that were used to assist us with a better understanding of the objective being taught.

The characteristic most exhibited by Mrs. Isabella was that she had her own unique personal touch to certain things and situations. She connected with each student as an individual and as a group. She also got involved in the school and with all the students attending the school. Mrs. Isabella was one of those teachers who did not mind giving a helping hand.

During my school days, I was involved in a lot of extracurricular activities. During this time, it was basketball season and I was a new cheerleader. My mother was a single parent who really did not have time to get off work and come to each and every event I was involved with. I can remember the first home game of the season was on a Friday night. My mother could not make it that night because she had to work. It was the grand opening of the season. The basketball players and cheerleaders would be introduced for the first time to the home crowd.

That Friday before the game, I remember sitting at my desk with my head between my hands. I was crying so much, that Mrs. Isabella came and asked what was troubling me? I told her and she just gave me a great big hug.

At the end of the school day, I prepared for the game. I did not know whether to feel happy or sad. As I was being introduced as a new cheerleader, I looked into the audience and to my surprise, I saw Mrs. Isabella standing and cheering for me! My frown turned into a great big smile.

After the game, I ran up to Mrs. Isabella and gave her a great big hug and told her thank you. She replied, "No, thank you! I treat you and all of my students like you are my own children." Therefore, I nominate Mrs. Isabella as the most effective and inspiring teacher of my lifetime.

Your Secret "Edmirer"
by
Amy Newsom

Mrs. Woodruff was my fourth grade teacher at Meadowview Elementary School in Selma, Alabama. She was the most effective teacher I had throughout my elementary school years for many reasons. One of her greatest assets as a teacher was her ability to give teaching a personal touch.

Mrs. Woodruff did an incredible job at making me feel special. I loved Mrs. Woodruff so much that I would often leave pictures that I had drawn for her on her desk when she was not looking. I would label them, "From your secret 'edmirer'." She knew that these gifts were from me, because she knew that I could not correctly spell 'admirer.' Instead of making me feel stupid because I was a very poor speller, she just laughed. She made me believe that I was cute and funny instead of silly and dumb. Mrs. Woodruff was one of the key adults from my childhood that helped to sculpt my self-concept in a positive manner.

V-Day Treat
by
Jarita Berry

I believe that the most powerful trait that a teacher can contribute to any classroom is the ability to bring a personal touch into that classroom. For me, it was my third and fourth grade teacher. Her name was Ms. Lori Lockheart, and she taught at Oak Park Elementary School in Aurora, Illinois. Before understanding how this one lady changed my life, one must understand the neighborhood. Oak Park rested in the heart of the second largest city in Illinois, and many of the children attending the school came from dysfunctional backgrounds. Many of these students were afraid to learn, care, and even be themselves.

Ms. Lockheart showed that it was okay to be yourself. She did this through various activities. She established this fact on the first day of school. She decorated the room using her own creativity. She did it by using pictures, drawings, and other items made by previous students. As the year progressed, she replaced the previous students' artwork with ours.

As the year continued, she visited some of our homes. The homes that she picked were the "at-risk" students, but we did not know that we were classified as such. She allowed us to pick different V-Day (Victory Day) treats from a box. My V-Day treat was to go with her to eat ice cream after school. I was able to pick my best friend to come with me.

Ms. Lockheart did not call my mother to ask permission to take me and my best friend out for ice cream. She paid my mother a visit. During the visit, she discussed different issues concerning me. She also gave me much praise. After the meeting, I was taken to Baskin Robins. Ms. Lockheart really took the time to show me just how much she cared.

The Teacher With An Exotic Look
by
Meredith Wade

One of my elementary school teachers that I adored the most was my sixth grade Language Arts teacher, Mrs. Fran Bond. Mrs. Bond had a very unique and exotic look to her, which intrigued all the students. She had solid, long black hair that came all the way down her back. She was part Cherokee Indian and she went all out on tribal events, culture, and readings. I remember reading and dissecting the tribal literature for meaning. This is just another way she exposed us to different types of literature, word meaning, and culture. She took great pride in her culture and her heritage.

Mrs. Bond influenced me in so many ways that year. I recently had the honor and privilege of being her colleague. When I took my first long-term substitute teaching job in 2003, she was teaching at the school were I was hired. Ironically enough, she was the pair teacher of my mother that year and had been keeping up with me all those years through my mother. I hope that I have the same characteristics and impact on my students that Mrs. Bond had on me all these years. I will never forget how special she made me feel. I hope to pass that feeling on to my students.

Feeling Like I've Been Visited by the President of the United States
by
Rebecca Wingo

I will always remember my fourth grade teacher, Mrs. Mosely. She was pretty, soft spoken, always seemed to enjoy what she was doing, and genuinely seemed to care about each one of her students.

It was my first year at Sacred Heart School. I had gone to a different private school from kindergarten to third grade and even though I knew many of the children in my class from church, it was still a new environment and experience. I was very self-conscious, but Mrs. Mosely took me under her wings and made the transition as easy as possible.

She was the type of teacher who was always telling stories about her life now and when she was a child. She had no children of her own so we always felt like her children. She also gave us time to share our ideas, thoughts, and stories. She was the type of teacher who made the extra effort to make each student feel like an important part of the class. She also made a point to go and see each student at sporting or after school events. I was playing soccer at that time and remember the day she came to watch me play.

I was very excited that she was coming. I remember being on the field during warm ups and seeing her walk up to the field. I smiled and she waved at me. I waved back. I don't remember anything about the game itself or who won. What I do remember is looking over to the sideline and seeing her there and feeling very special and important. After the game, she gave me a big hug before she left. I felt like the President of the United States had just watched me play—what an incredible feeling!

There are still teachers today who take the time and make the commitment to add these personal touches for their students throughout the school year. My own children have all had the great experience of having several teachers who went that extra mile. I hope it made them feel just as important as I did all those years ago when Mrs. Mosely came to my soccer game.

A Teacher and Friend
by
Jennifer Cupples

What makes an effective teacher? This is the question I asked myself before writing this assignment. To me an effective teacher is someone who adds a personal touch. It is important because during K-12 school years, children need something more than just learning Math and English. They need someone who they feel really understands them. If they do not have that sense of security then it is a lot harder to reach them during these important years.

My most effective teacher was my fifth grade teacher, Mrs. Rogers. Mrs. Rogers was a wonderful teacher, she not only taught us the fundamentals we needed in order to step up into the big world of middle school; she also made an effort to get to know each child. She was the teacher who would come to your birthday party and help you celebrate. This was very important to every 10 year old. She also made an effort to come to all school activities whether they were during school or after school. She would even eat with us during lunch and share stories and encourage us to share also.

Mrs. Rogers was very important to me because this was an exceptionally hard time for me. I was fairly new to the school and I had not grown up there so I did not have the friends that the other students had. I also was going through a hard time with my parents being divorced.

Mrs. Rogers made an effort to understand what I was going through. She talked with my mom to see if there was anything she could do. She also helped me make friends by introducing me to her son that was in the same grade but in a different class. This allowed me to meet people I might never have met. Now that I am older, I feel that Mrs. Rogers helped me more than I could have imagined. Not only was she a good teacher, she was also a good friend.

Comforted Me Like A Mother
by
Natasha S. Walton

An effective teacher is one who runs an effective classroom, and touches the lives of children. During my eight grade year, Mrs. Glover made tremendous impacts on my life that helped mold me into what I am today. I feel that she went beyond the call of duty and really cared for me. During my parent's divorce, Mrs. Glover comforted me like a mother. She saw that my grades were dropping and offered extra help to bring them back up. There wasn't a day that went by that she didn't offer a helping hand. She connected with me in a personal and professional way.

Mrs. Glover would call if I missed a day of school. This showed me how concerned she was. Being a teenager, my self-esteem was lowered because my parents had divorced, and I had no school spirit. She lifted my spirits and instilled in me that the world was not over. She told me I should hold my head up high because someone was going through something worse than me.

Mrs. Glover is the teacher that I'm becoming. I want to be an effective teacher with all 12 characteristics an effective teacher has. When I become a teacher and have taught long enough for the students to reach college, I want my students to think of me as an effective teacher and a great role model. I want to be a great asset to my students like Mrs. Glover was to me.

Develops a Sense of Belonging

Develops a Sense of Belonging – Effective teachers have a way of making students feel welcomed and comfortable in their classrooms.

✓ One thing repeatedly mentioned by students was the fact that they felt like they belonged in the classroom taught by an effective teacher.

✓ The students felt that the teacher was happy to have them in the classroom.

Students have a need to fit in—to relate. Belonging refers to finding one's place in the classroom—to feeling welcomed. It has to do with a student feeling that he or she fits into the learning environment.

In order for a student to have a sense of belonging, that student must first feel that the teacher is happy to have him or her in the classroom. Also, the student does not sense that he or she is being treated unfairly.

The simple task of welcoming students at the door each day, speaking to them, saying good morning, and calling students by name is an excellent way to develop in students a sense of belonging:

"Mary, how has your day been?"

"Good morning Thaddeus, did you have a good weekend?"

"Hello, Hosea, did your soccer team win the game last night?"

Children, like adults, have a strong psychological and emotional need to feel significant, important, and appreciated. They need to feel that they are valuable and have a place in the classroom world. They also need to feel that they can be helpful to others and are an asset to the classroom.

Children who feel valued and competent are more likely to be positive about life in general and will do well in school. A healthy sense of their own personal self-worth also helps children be more open to people from other backgrounds because they are less likely to fear differences or put other children down to feel better about themselves (Smith, 2004).

Having a *Sense of Belonging* is especially needed during the adolescent years when peer pressure is usually at its peak. This stage of life is strongly influenced by children's social groups and the media. As educators, we must build a classroom climate that gives a sense of family.

Your classroom should be one that encourages positive relationships among students. A classroom where students know each others' names and see each other as human beings—is a classroom where traits such as compassion, kindness, empathy, helpfulness, caring, cooperation, loyalty, tolerance, and respect will be manifested on a daily basis. This positive climate will meet students' need for love and the sense of belonging—even if they are not receiving it at home.

Your classroom can be an escape from the harsh realities of life. This sense of belonging in your classroom will in turn create a positive learning environment where students can interact with peers to accomplish the academic goals of the classroom. The more students feel that they are a welcomed part of the classroom, the more they will be willing to take risks, confront each other in a positive way, and speak up about issues that are important to them. The best learning takes place in a positive, social environment were children feel a sense of belonging.

Small collaborative group activities, in which each child is assigned a specific responsibility in the group, are excellent ways for you to increase students' sense of belonging in your classroom. Whether circle time for young children or a group project for high school students, these community building activities give students opportunities to interact with each other in an enjoyable way while reaching the educational objectives.

Everyone needs a friend. Therefore, these activities can help students from different socioeconomic and cultural backgrounds to better understand and befriend one another. As they interact, they will be better able to see things from the other person's point of view.

Although it is very important that, as a teacher, you develop a classroom climate where students respect and care for each other, the critical component for having a classroom that develops a sense of belonging is you—the teacher. It's also very important for the students to feel they can relate successfully with you.

If a student feels that he can't approach you or that you don't care about him and do not want him in your classroom, or if you display a "get out of my face!" attitude towards the student, that student may achieve his need for a sense of belonging by misbehaving. The student may misbehave so he can obtain a sense of belonging by being dubbed the class clown or bully—or he may act up so that he can be placed in another classroom where he *will* feel safe and accepted.

As educators, the more we encourage students, the less they will choose to misbehave. Why? Because the more we encourage them, the more their self-esteem will grow. Students with higher self-esteem have a tendency to achieve more. Positive reinforcement breeds positive behavior. Negative reinforcement leads to anger, frustration, and a feeling of powerlessness. These feelings often erupt in inappropriate behaviors—especially in adolescents who may have never learned appropriate means of dealing with such emotions. School violence may be the end results of students who do not have a sense of belonging.

As an educator, it's important that you help every student feel that she or he is a vital part of your classroom. Something as simple as saying to a student, "Welcome back Michelle. I missed you yesterday," can go a long way in letting a student know that she is wanted in your classroom and that someone actually notices her, and cares about her.

Your positive relationship with students, especially your most difficult students, will help every student in your classroom to form positive relationships with you and with one another. Your actions will be a living role model to your students as to how they should deal positively with a difficult person.

Celebrate the uniqueness and diversity of your students. Allow all students to contribute to the class in their own unique ways. Every morning when students greet each other, share thoughts or do character building activities together. Make a concerted effort to decrease negative cliques from forming in your classroom.

Daily stride to increase students' sense of belonging and togetherness (Brick, 2002). Work to make all children feel that your classroom is their family and a place where they can feel safe. The following essays speak of educators who developed a wonderful Sense of Belonging in their classrooms.

The Man I Fell In Love With
by
Angela L. Robinson

My most effective teacher (K-6) was Mr. Banker at Patterson Elementary. Mr. Banker taught 5th grade mathematics, science and social studies. He was an effective teacher in my life because he brought out the best in each of his students. I loved him because he made me feel good about myself. Mr. Banker was a compassionate man whom I looked up to very much. Years after leaving, I return to Patterson Elementary just to see him.

When I was in the 5th grade, my mother would stay out a lot partying. Well, she would come home very late in the night. So; when it was time for my brothers and me to get ready for school the next morning, she would not get out of bed to get us ready. I missed several days from school that year and my peers would tease me saying, "You are going to flunk because you missed too many days." Mr. Banker did not allow that to happen. He would always teach me the objectives I missed.

Even though I missed so many days, I managed to earn honor roll every nine weeks. In addition to that, I had very low self-esteem. I sucked my thumb. I had crooked front teeth. I always held my head down, was soft spoken and I dragged my feet when I walked. Mr. Baker was a father to me that year and I fell in love with him. I fell in love with a white, over six feet tall man who helped me to gain confidence in myself. He was there for me in a time of my life when it was very hard. My mother thought her life was more important than raising her children. At the end of my 5th grade year, I went to live with my grandmother. Mr. Banker helped me to love school and that is why I believe he was my most effective teacher.

He Helped Me To Feel Like I Belonged
by
Shannon Colombini Morgan

I attended a magnet school. My favorite teacher was Coach Moore. I had him as a P.E. teacher in 8th and 9th grade. In this P.E. class—we did P.E.! It was not free play time. Coach Moore developed a sense of belonging in the classroom. For example, at the beginning of class we had to exercise. If any person did it sloppy, he made all of us do it over until he felt we did it correctly. He called each of us his 'fatheads.' He treated everybody the same. But most importantly, he helped me to feel like I belonged. I had gone to a very small private school for a little over 6 years. In the middle of my 7th grade year, I switched to a big public school where I didn't know a soul. It was very upsetting. Everybody had grown up with everybody else and they already had their cliques. Being the new kid — nobody really opened up to me. Then my parents decided to apply for the magnet school. I was accepted. Right before I started, suddenly and unexpectedly, my grandfather was killed in a car wreck. I was very close to him, and really thought my world was shattered. Needless to say, when I went to school, my life to me had changed so much and I didn't really feel like I belonged.

When I started Baldwin Magnet School, I had Coach Moore first thing in the morning. He developed a classroom community where he actually listened to his students. He listened to my story about my grandfather and offered advice on how to get through something like that. Having Coach Moore as a teacher helped me to feel like I belonged again.

The Crazy Lady!
by
Nancy Stewart

As I sat and reminisced about which one of my past teachers had the most impact on my life, I realized this was a very hard task. There were some pretty good teachers in my past. Yet, I vaguely remember their names. So, I figured these teachers could not have been all that great if I cannot remember their names. However, when I think about my last few years of school, I found myself thinking about how difficult high school was for me and most other students. The more I thought about how challenging high school became year after year, one teacher began to stick out in my mind.

Mrs. Martha Williams was an eleventh grade American History teacher. Everyone thought she was the craziest teacher on the school campus. She would come to school on Fridays dressed in a long khaki shirt, a green and white C. F. Vigor High School shirt, white tennis shoes, green and white socks, and she would have two green and white cheerleader pom-poms in her hands. She felt as if every Friday was Spirit Day.

At the time, we did not know why Mrs. Williams dressed that way or shook her pom-poms so wildly down the school halls. The more I think about those days, I realized it was more than her encouraging students to win on the football field, basketball court, track and field, or in any other sport; it was Mrs. Williams' creative way of encouraging us to win in life. I can remember Mrs. Williams each day encouraging the students in and out of her class to always do their best. If you participated in an athletic sport or not, she still felt that each student had a sense of belonging in her classroom as well as the entire school. She told us, "You all have an important purpose in life and it is outside these school walls."

There was this one particular time I saw her talking to one of our star football players outside in the hallway. I overheard her ask that student an important question: "What are you going to do if you do not receive a football scholarship?" I am not sure what else she told him after that, but it was not long after that conversation that I saw that star player coming to school on time and studying his work each day. The compassion Mrs. Williams showed that student changed his life.

When I took Mrs. Williams' class, I had the same idea about her as any other student—"this lady is crazy!" Now, being a teacher myself, I understand she acted that way to get our attention. Her creativity, sense of belonging, and compassion had a huge impact on all those students that attended C. F Vigor High School. She will never be forgotten and will always be a perfect example of being an effective teacher.

A New Family
by
Jacqueline Means

When I think of the most effective teacher in my life, there is no doubt in my mind that Ms. Pamela Tucker fits that description. Ms. Tucker was my sixth grade teacher. The very first day of class, she went over all her rules. To my surprise, her rules were not the usual long list of don'ts I had become accustomed to. Her rules resembled today's character education lessons.

She told all of us to look around the room, and then she said, with a big welcoming smile, "This is your new family." Ms. Tucker introduced herself formally to the class then gave each student the opportunity to do the same. She would then tell us the characteristics of a family. She said things like protecting, caring, sharing, helping, being considerate, and respecting each other.

One of the most unforgettable moments for me happened when I was sitting in my desk very quietly while the rest of the class was interacting. After this took place for a couple of days, Ms. Tucker came and pulled a chair beside my desk and said, in a very personal tone, "I've noticed you sitting by yourself all the time. Is everything alright?" I answered, "Yes," shyly. Then she said, "If you are having a problem with some of the children brothering you or anything please let me know, because I really want you to be happy in my class, okay!"

Hearing her say that gave me a very comforting feeling because never before had a teacher expressed concern about my happiness. I soon noticed that she demonstrated that same concern for all of her students. Her positive attitude must have rubbed off on all of us because we had a tendency to show concern for our classmates, too. At that point in my life, I stopped believing things people said about others without proof because Ms. Tucker was far from the monster that other students portrayed her to be. She was truly the most compassionate teacher, and it was a blessing to be in her class!

A Lesson in Crying
by
Pedro Lewis

In 1962, I had the pleasure of meeting Mrs. Dorothy Posey Jones, my second grade teacher. During that year she became aware of my difficulty with word recognition. I can recall sitting in her class feeling all alone because I felt I didn't have the knowledge of many of the other children. Each student would be assigned five sight words for homework.

The next morning, the students would be selected to go to the word wall to recite and identify the five words they were assigned. I remember this as if it were yesterday. Mrs. Jones called on me to recite and identify my words. I was able to pronounce one or two of the words. One word that stands out most clearly was "cry."

For a minute or two, I stood there unable to pronounce the word, but it seemed like an hour. The class began to laugh uncontrollably, and she quickly directed the children to stop laughing, but by this time, I was crying and wanted to sit down. I recall her telling the class this is a learning environment, and there would be no laughing at anyone. After the class had become quiet, she asked me what was I doing and my reply was, "crying." She stated that the word was cry. At that point in my life I realized she was a kind person who cared about me.

Mrs. Jones took an interest in other students as well—to make sure they had the skills needed to become effective readers. I recall her taking three or four students from the regular classroom setting and working with us for 30 minutes or more each day. Mrs. Jones was a compassionate teacher, because she had a passion for teaching and learning.

Ides of March
by
Jackie Kilpatrick

My favorite teacher was Mrs. Ruth Hill at Stanhope Elmore High School. Mrs. Hill taught Latin to me in the ninth and tenth grades. Mrs. Hill was my favorite teacher because she was positive, prepared, and gave me a sense of belonging.

Mrs. Hill was by far the most positive teacher I had while at Stanhope Elmore. During the first year of Latin, I really struggled to learn the different verb endings, and the masculine and feminine endings. My freshman year I had a solid 'C' in her class and did not want to take the second semester, especially the second year of Latin. Mrs. Hill encouraged me every day, telling me that I was getting it and the second year would be easier. She was right, the second year I earned an 'A.'

Latin class for Mrs. Hill was a way of life. She loved the Romans and their language and taught us to love them too. We celebrated all of the Roman holidays with feasts and parties. I expected us to have lions and Christians before the year was out. On the Ides of March (March 15) we mourned the death of Julius Caesar. We held a funeral each year and she gave a very touching eulogy that had all the girls crying and even the boys wiping their eyes. We teased her by rhyming, "That Latin is a dead language, as dead as it can be. It killed all the Romans and now it is killing me." Mrs. Hill would smile and keep on teaching.

Mrs. Hill made me feel totally at home in her class. I knew I would be treated fairly and was loved by her. I don't know how she did it, but everyone in her class felt like the teacher's pet. Many years after we graduated, several of us were discussing her class and each of us felt that we were her pet. Then we realized that somehow she had made all of us feel special. When she walked down the hall, former students were always hugging and speaking to her. She was a very popular teacher. I loved her class and I loved her.

Mrs. Hill was a positive teacher, was always prepared to make us love the Romans and made us feel a sense of belonging in her class. Even though she taught me Latin, I can look at almost any English word and tell you the meaning because many of our words come from Latin. I was able to tell her, before she died, what a difference she had made in my life. She seemed pleased to have made a difference in me and I hope one day to return her kindnesses to my students by using her as my role model.

A Concerned Friend
by
Ronnie Allen Doughty

When it comes to thinking about my favorite teacher, many names come to mind. The qualities that attract me to these teachers are their willingness to teach, the connection they build between their students, and their caring personalities. Most people don't notice their favorite teacher until much later in their school career, but it was quite different with me. I had the great pleasure of meeting my favorite teacher during my first year in school. Yeah, that's right, kindergarten!

Mr. Ricky Farmer was one of two kindergarten teachers at Davis Elementary School. Also, he was one of the few Caucasian teachers at this majority black school and one of a handful of male kindergarten teachers in the school district. I remember Mr. Farmer just as if it were yesterday! I remember walking into his class on the first day of school. His room was very colorful with various learning centers just waiting for children to come and explore them. In fact, Mr. Farmer really believed in creativity as a form of learning. He believed that creativity was the basis for learning. Also, he was very involved in the lives of each of his students and would never break promises that he made with his students.

Mr. Farmer had many characteristics that I would like to discuss, but his main quality was how his students developed a sense of belonging. Mr. Farmer was more than just a teacher. He was a concerned friend. This is very important when it comes to teaching kindergarteners. Usually, it's very hard to connect with a small child.

Mr. Farmer was great with helping children to express themselves at a very early age. In fact, my mother used to think it was hilarious how I would try to solve her problems and talk to her about expressing herself to me. Just think, a 5-year-old wanting to have an adult conversation. I really think this is what created the foundation for my caring personality.

Mr. Farmer also did not mind getting down on the floor to play with his students. He really explored our lives from top to bottom. A good teacher does not mind working hands-on with his or her students. This really shows that they care, not only about our education, but our well being. While having center time, Mr. Farmer would visit each center with the students occupying it. He would play whatever the students were playing, and actually enjoyed it!

The best thing about this teacher was that he never broke his promises to students. For instance, he promised us a trip to the zoo. For weeks he asked parents to become volunteers for our trip. Only two parents signed up and 20 children could not fit into two cars. So, instead of canceling the trip, Mr. Farmer called his mother, father, and brother to help. His family stepped in and saved the day! They volunteered their time and drove us to the zoo. His family did not just volunteer once, they did it the entire year out of the goodness of their hearts.

As one can see, Mr. Farmer really developed a sense of belonging with his students. As kindergarten students, we knew that our teacher really cared about us. In fact, this sense of belonging encompassed every other aspect within the classroom. It taught us to care for our classroom and to keep it tidy. Also, every child wanted to please the teacher both academically and socially. Last, but not least, Mr. Farmer's sense of belonging approach reduced discipline problems in the classroom. Everyone was too busy trying to do his or her very best at everything he wanted us to do. His classroom environment was like a family. We cared for one another and respected each other. I have always described Mr. Farmer as a bright and shining star in the classroom, and I hope I will have some of his many unique qualities when I become an educator.

May you rest in peace, Mr. Farmer.

The Black Bird Group
by
Jennifer S. Miller

Everyone has that one special teacher who impacts their life so profoundly that words cannot express their true meaning within our lives. For me, her name was Debra Bentley and she came at a time when I could not have needed her more. Like many children of divorced parents, I always felt caught in the middle. Even though my parents had been divorced for several years, I decided to live with my Dad for a while. Mrs. Bentley showed me many things about myself that I still hold dear today.

All alone, at a new school, I had no sense of belonging. Also, the system I moved to seemed to be much further ahead in the curriculum and I already felt as if I were behind. Even in third grade, I was struggling with reading and everyone had given me the label of being in the Black Bird Group (you know the group). All my reservations did not affect nor hinder Mrs. Bentley. It was almost like I became her masterpiece that she would work on day-after-day until it was perfected. There were times in class when all I could do was stare at her in amazement because things finally "clicked."

She took the time to uncover my reading difficulties on her own. She then initiated the tests that led to the discovery of my dyslexia. So many before her had simply labeled me and sent me on my way. Imagine my surprise the day she informed me that I wasn't slow, I was a gifted student who simply had a little trouble with letters.

To put it quite honestly, I owe my life to her. Defeat is no longer a word in my vocabulary. I think about her often and wish she could see me with my students. The desire to please her and meet her expectations still drives me. When I have students who need extra care and attention, I just remember when I was in their place, and all those emotions come flooding back. Teaching is an art where one must educate the whole child. I am learning that more and more everyday.

A Place In The Heart
by
Heather Miller

When I reflect back on my years of schooling, one teacher sticks out in my mind. Her name was Mrs. Broderick at Head Elementary School. She was my first grade teacher. She had many of the 12 characteristics but the one I remember most was that she gave all of us a true sense of belonging. From the moment we entered her classroom, she made us feel like we were welcomed and that she was so excited we were there. Everyone had a specific job to do everyday and she made us feel like no one else was "qualified" to do our job. And she made us feel like our job was the most important job in the world. Everyone really got to know each other, too. We would switch tables every week until we had sat with everyone in our class and we were all friends. I also remember that whenever we were absent from school, she would call us to make sure we were okay and she would let us know that everyone missed us.

Even though I remember all of the fun and creative things we did and how sweet and happy she was, what I remember the most was the feeling that I was in the right place. Going into first grade from kindergarten was very scary for me but Mrs. Broderick made me feel like everything was going to be fine. I felt that I really belonged in first grade and in her class.

In my own classroom, I try to make my students feel that same sense of belonging. I use many of Mrs. Broderick's ideas like putting my students' names everywhere in my room and decorating the room with all of their artwork. I also allow my students to come up with our classroom rules. It frustrates me when I hear other teachers saying "MY classroom." I always refer to the room as "OUR classroom." This really makes the students take ownership of the classroom and feel a sense of pride in keeping it tidy and clean. Mrs. Broderick is not teaching at Head anymore but I know that her gentle and happy spirit still has a place in the hearts of all of her former students.

Teacher's Pet
by
Sophronia Towles

My most effective teacher was in elementary school. I attended Fairfax Elementary and Mrs. Jennifer Wooley was my fifth and sixth grade teacher. The reason I had her both fifth and sixth grade was because she moved up a grade after my fifth grade year. She was truly a wonderful lady. Some would say that I was the teacher's pet. Mrs. Wooley always told the class that she was getting old and did not remember where she put things. Mrs. Wooley always depended on me to help her find things in her classroom. She could always just look at me and I would tell her exactly where she put something. She often told me that I could spot a spider crawling up the wall. That was her way of telling me that I was very observant.

Mrs. Wooley told her class on day one to always tell her the truth about whatever we did whether it was right or wrong and she would back us up on the situation. This has been something that has stuck with me all my life. It did not necessarily matter to her what we did as long as we told the truth about it. This helped me to build character and I tell my students the same thing today.

Mrs. Wooley believed in all her students and was always loving and concerned about us. She developed cancer at the end of fifth grade and I was so worried about her but she fought the odds and pulled through. At our sixth grade graduation, Mrs. Wooley asked me to do the graduation speech and I accepted. I could see just how proud of me she was at the end of graduation. I have a caring spirit towards my students today because of this effective teacher that I had in elementary school. She wanted to make sure that all of her students were given 100 percent of her on a daily basis. Mrs. Wooley instilled in me character as well as the trait to be an effective teacher.

The Funny Talking Kid
by
Jamie Holloway

My most effective teacher was Mrs. Combs. She was my third grade teacher in Slidell, Louisiana at Little Oak Elementary School. She taught math, science and social studies. Her best characteristic was that she made me feel as though I belonged in her class and as if I had been there the whole year. She developed in me the sense of belonging.

In January of 1990, my family and I relocated to Slidell, Louisiana, from San Francisco, California. My father was in the Navy at the time and he was told he would be stationed in New Orleans, Louisiana. My mother, brother and I had never lived anywhere outside of California so we were reluctant to move.

When we arrived in Louisiana, the school system was extremely different. Upon my arrival, Mrs. Combs made me feel as though I had been in her class the whole school year. She knew that I felt out of place because people were laughing at the way I spoke. Many kids said that I talked as though I were "white." Mrs. Combs overheard the others and explained to the class that people from different parts of the United States have different dialects so students should not expect everyone they meet to sound or even look a certain way.

Mrs. Combs also made me feel as though I belonged in her classroom. She offered me extra help to catch me up on my math skills. In California, we were just learning our multiplication facts, but in Louisiana, the students were already on division. I was extremely lost and frustrated. Mrs. Combs sent home extra math work and also gave me one-on-one tutoring while the remainder of the class was doing their work independently.

Mrs. Combs showed me the sense of belonging. She made me feel special and allowed me to feel 100 percent a part of her third grade class in Slidell, Louisiana.

It Was a Science Thing
by
Sussie Prater

I attended Citronelle High School in Citronelle, Alabama. The school I attended was predominately white and the racial tension was high. The majority of my teachers were Caucasian. My favorite teacher was Coach Walding. He was the tennis coach and taught many of the science classes. He made the classroom come alive. Chemistry wasn't my best subject, but he made it interesting. My favorite subject that I took from him was anatomy and physiology. Instead of listening to a boring lecture, he was more hands-on. We dissected different body parts of animals. Once we discovered the different parts and functions, he let us free. By free, I mean if we wanted to mutilate the rest of the project, then we could.

The projects and labs were always partner related. Being in a diverse school environment, the group work allowed us to bond more. It wasn't a black and white thing, but a science thing. Everyone was on one accord with the lesson and unconcerned with the skin color of the person sitting beside them. I never sensed favoritism in the classroom. His positive attitude and enthusiasm inspired me and made learning fun.

I tell my students that I will not sit and lecture, because I would put myself to sleep. I try my best to liven up the learning environment. My students enjoy performing hands-on activities.

Coach Walding also taught me that being prepared can make the class hour run smoothly. Group activities are my favorite teaching pastimes because the children learn so much from each other. Coach Walding was young and caring amongst the students. I see myself in the same light as Coach Walding. I am young and I hope to leave an impression upon my students. His teaching style has had a lasting impression on my life. I appreciate him for being my teacher.

Playing the Xylophone
by
Keisha Cooper

The most effective teacher in my life that I remember was my sixth grade music teacher, Mr. Larson, at Lincoln Elementary School in Plant City, Florida. I lived across the street from my school and would always see Mr. Larson arriving at school before any of the other teachers and principal, and he would always be the last to leave.

Mr. Larson was a kind, fair, and productive man. He was also very funny. Mr. Larson took time out to teach those students who didn't understand music very well but was still interested in learning. I first learned to read music in Mr. Larson's class, which prompted me to be in the band for the next three years in junior high, where I played the xylophone.

Mr. Larson was very effective in my life because he had a lot of patience. He would spend a lot of time with us, and you could tell that his concern for the students was genuine and not "temporary." Certain teachers only cared enough while they were at school, and at 3:15 p.m., they would be the first out the door.

I am an educator now and I have the same kind of patience and love that Mr. Larson had for me. I am patient with my students, and I go the extra mile with them because I know that at home many students do not receive the love and attention that they sometimes need.

I am very proud to be an educator. In my opinion, there are a lot of paycheck teachers today, and not enough of Mr. Larsons. I was blessed to have such a wonderful teacher, and I hope that I am making an impact on the students that I teach today, the same as Mr. Larson did for me—and I still like playing the xylophone.

A Place Where I Belonged
by
Justin Cooley

Although a very long time ago, I remember a teacher who displayed the characteristics of an effective teacher. After my father passed away, I found myself in a different state in a new school, Munson Elementary, in Milton, Florida, with a new teacher; her name was Mrs. Overstreet. It was my first grade year and I had missed a lot of time due to the funeral and move. Not knowing any of the other students or what to expect, I was a nervous wreck and scared to speak to anyone. I remember from the beginning how she introduced herself with a hug. It was as if she knew I had been through a lot and was letting me know it would be alright. Thinking back, what she did next was rather unusual, yet helped in ways I am still pondering. She continued with the lesson without introducing me. She introduced me at a later moment but at the time I believe she did not want to draw attention to a very scared little boy. She did not have any idea at that time just how far behind the other students I was due to the time lost. So, she refrained from asking me questions from any of the lessons during the day. In private, though, she would ask me questions from different subject areas. No matter what I said, she seemed happy about it. By the end of the day, she had gathered a small stack of books and papers on her desk and told me that she had arranged to drive me home. During the day I had a chance to slowly meet some of the students and even played with a few during recess, which helped me to not feel quite so nervous about being in a new place with strangers.

During the last part of the day, Mrs. Overstreet decided it was time to make introductions. First, all of the students had taken turns saying their names and stating something unique about themselves. When it was my turn, I thought she would blurt out that my father had died, but what she did was more surprising. After saying my name, she told the children that my family was a part of the military and that we had lived in places they may have never heard of. Until the bell rang to go home, I regaled everyone with our exploits of living in Guam and the Philippines. After everyone left, Mrs. Overstreet let me help her gather stuff together and carry it to her truck.

On the short trip to my home, she asked me how my day went. She then told me she knew what it was like to be the new person and how scary it can be but I shouldn't be scared because we are all new at some time. When we reached my grandparent's home, she spoke with my mother concerning the material I needed to learn in order to catch up with the others.

I remember there were times after school she would work with me to help me understand various concepts. It did not take me long to become just one of the students, which made me very happy. It may sound like I am writing about her compassion, her personal touch, her positive attitude, or her high expectations, and you would be right. She did have these qualities and more. She ultimately helped me to feel safe and like I belonged there. The characteristic of my most effective teacher was to help me develop a sense of belonging. From that day forth, I always felt that Mrs. Overstreet's classroom was where I belonged when I was not at home.

Characteristic #8

Admits Mistakes

Admits Mistakes – Effective teachers are quick to apologize to students when an error was made.

✓ Example (1): When a student is mistakenly accused, the teacher is willing to apologize to the student.

✓ Example (2): The teacher is willing to make adjustments when students inform the teacher that there was mate-rial on the test they were not told to study or when errors are made in grading.

✓ Example (3): The teacher is willing to give students an opportunity to redo a project if she did not explain an important step in the assignment.

Teachers are humans, and humans make mistakes, such as losing your cool or saying something to a student that you really didn't mean to say, or making a mistake while teaching a concept to your students. You should really try to keep these to a minimum. But when you do make a mistake, it is important to admit your error. If the mistake was made in public, the apology should be given in public. If you embarrassed or wrongfully accused a student in front of the class, then you should apologize in front of the class—not by calling the student out in the hall and privately apologizing (Walters, 2004).

If you are a new teacher, you may (like I did) come into the teaching profession with the *Super Teacher* complex—thinking that you can do no wrong! You may think that you are going to save the day for all the children you teach, they are going to appreciate you as their superhero, sit and listen to everything you have to say, and be obedient and respond by saying, "Oh yes, my great and noble teacher—teacher me! I will listen! I will learn!"

But now that you are in the classroom—just you and those twenty-or-so beautiful little faces staring back at you—you know that some of them, for whatever reason, couldn't care less about what you have to say. As a result, you may expect too much of yourself and think that you should not make any mistakes. Or worse yet, think that you have already made the biggest mistake of your life—becoming a teacher!

Perhaps you thought that your college degree would be enough for you to walk into the classroom and teach without any problems and without making mistakes. However, you are now mindful of the fact that the teaching profession and the classroom experience, are, for the most part, totally different than your college experience. Making mistakes are a part of the learning process in becoming an effective teacher.

You should not feel ashamed or defensive about revealing or admitting your mistakes. You should work with a mentor in order to improve in the areas where you are having problems and learn from your mistakes. Always try to do better the next time.

Don't be intimidated by a student who points out a mistake you made or who thinks he knows more than you do. Just say, "Thank you Johnny for noticing that error. I am glad you are paying attention!" and then continue with the lesson.

If students are constantly complaining that they don't understand your teaching methods or that your class is boring—you should listen. Perhaps there is some truth in what they are saying. Sometimes children can be brutally honest (more honest than your coworkers), and they may not care about hurting your feelings. So take heed to what they are saying to you and about you. If students can't learn the way you teach, then you should teach the way they learn.

It's very important to realize that nobody's perfect and that even the most experienced teacher in your school makes mistakes. Don't be afraid to ask for help and invite constructive criticism from a trusted coworker. Use your mistakes as an opportunity to develop problem solving techniques. Remember that Thomas Edison, the inventor of the light bulb, made hundreds of mistakes in his experimenting on the light bulb before he found the method that worked. You should place the same emphasis on becoming an effective teacher. "Growth begins when we accept our own weakness" (Vanier, 2005 p.1).

Baby Making Machines
by
Omeisha Hargrove

> *There are times when students will take extremely negative comments that a teacher made to them and turn them into something positive—as you will see in this next essay.*

From day one in Ms. B's class at Tilson Elementary in Decatur, Georgia, I knew that with her as my teacher it was going to be a very interesting school year. As the year progressed, I noticed how her patience with me wore very thin, especially whenever I raised my hand or wanted to participate. She seemed to ignore me or give me an intimidating look. As a child, all I wanted from her was attention. I tried very hard to be on my best behavior in her class. I disasso ciated myself from my friends in the class just so she would see that I was trying to become a better student. She was a well liked teacher by all my peers, but for some reason, I could never share in their excitement when it came to Ms. B.

Constantly being ignored in class and receiving what I thought was con-structive criticism, I never said anything to my parents because for a long time, I thought that I was doing something wrong. Well, yes, I talked a lot and I never did the work as she would tell me. But, the way she treated me and what she said to me was still inappropriate. It did not motivate me to want to do the work.

The night of our parent teacher conference, I hated the idea of my parents going to her room to hear the status of how I was doing in her class. After that night, my parents became a little bothered by how in all the other classes I was doing very well, but in her class it showed that I was on a 3rd grade level in the 5th grade. Whenever my mom asked her for a conference, she was never avail-able or it wasn't the right time.

Two weeks after the PTA meeting, my mother sent a note through me to give to Ms. B. My mother told me to give it to her at the end of class. I gave her the note as I was told. She looked at me and ripped up the note in front of my face. She told me that she didn't care what my mother had to say in that note, that my mother was wasting her time with me because I "acted too grown and don't know a child's place." She went on to say that little girls like me wouldn't grow up to amount to anything but "baby making machines." By then I was terrified. My eyes were full of tears.

Ms. B. told me that there was no need to cry because I brought this all on myself. As she was talking to me, I began to believe what she was saying. I went home, told my mother about the incident. My mom was not very happy with the comments made by Ms. B. The next day my mother had a talk with the principal and the teacher denied everything that was said. However, my home-room teacher had heard the entire conversation and had already reported the incident to the principal.

I was able to turn Ms. B's refusal to admit that she made a mistake in her judgment of me into something positive. Without her personal opinion on how my life would turn out, I would not be in the position I'm in today. Without her negative words of encouragement, I would not have graduated from high school with a 3.5 GPA, applied to college or be in preparation for graduating. Her lack of motivation gave me the incentive to do everything she told me I was not capable of doing—Thank you, Ms. B.!

Grammy Nomination
by
Marvin Borum

Being an effective teacher takes skills, knowledge, and continuous practice and therefore is not an easy task. For some teachers it may come naturally, while others may have to work at it to reach the effective status. Throughout my 18 years of school, I've experienced many different teachers with different teaching styles and certain characteristics of being effective. Among my experiences, I came across my greatest instructor, who indeed portrayed all the characteristics of being effective and made a difference in my life. My tenth grade biology teacher, Mrs. Ashayla Ford, is someone I can truly call an effective teacher.

She took time out and talked to any student she felt was having trouble with his/her work, in the home, at school in other classrooms, or wherever their problems may occur. She put herself in the student's shoes, letting him/her know that she had made the same mistakes before and that teachers aren't perfect. In her words, "We teachers aren't perfect and don't expect our students to be perfect, but at least learn from your mistakes."

If it were left up to me, I would give her a Grammy Nomination for best teacher ever.

Easing My Algebra Fears
by
Karen Lewis Dobbins

The teacher who made the most impact on me was Mrs. Adeline Parker. She was my 10th grade algebra teacher, and had it not been for her, I probably wouldn't have made it through algebra, nor would a lot of other students.

Mrs. Parker believed that each of her students could do algebra. She just had to find the switch that turned the light on for each student. She never belittled you or made you feel just plain dumb if you couldn't grasp a concept.

When Mrs. Parker could be proven wrong (that was not often) she had no problem admitting that she was wrong. She would always say, "We're all human and may make a mistake or two, but at least I know you understand this part because you can show me where I was wrong."

Mrs. Parker always had some type of "beginning" exercise that was used to introduce the new concept and would find other "easy" problems for those who needed to work on a lower level. She would consider the ability and feelings of her students when she did oral recitations or worked problems at the board. She would assign a problem that was equal to the ability of the student.

Don't Be a Statistic
by
Adrian Collins

One of my teachers who I feel has greatly contributed to my life was my 6th grade history teacher. Mr. Brinson was one of those teachers who showed tough love. He would tell you the things you needed to hear, not the things you wanted to hear. He would put you down in order to lift you up. He would admit when he made mistakes. Mr. Brinson was one of those teachers who would make you feel like you are on top of the world. He would help you with whatever was needed for you to be successful. He would tell you:

"You are not going to be anything."

"You are going to be just like the rest of the people who decided not to get an education, a statistic."

"Yeah, I guess you want a minimum wage job."

"I guess you want to work at the chicken house or the fish plant."

I know it sounds bad, but that's how he motivated us. After he gives his speech, you want to prove him wrong. You want him to know that you can be successful and not become a statistic. His saying at the end of each speech was, "You are what you think. So, if you think that you are a success, you are a success. But if you feel like a statistic, you are a statistic." He would tell us that it was okay to try to accomplish positive things and make mistakes. He would always say, "If you don't make mistakes, you will never know your weakness. It's your opportunity." So, that is why I feel that Mr. Brinson is my most effective teacher.

No Ones Perfect
by
Daphne M. McMillan

One characteristic of an effective teacher that appeals to me the most is being able to admit mistakes. A teacher who can admit a mistake is a teacher who will prove to have all the other characteristics.

I had a math teacher in the tenth grade who taught at a fast pace. She was the type who became angry if a person could not completely follow through with what she was teaching. Well, after a while all of her students grouped together to learn all the information we could before we went to class. On this particular day, we were going over homework in class, and I noticed that she had a couple of her answers wrong. At first I did not want to say anything, but I knew that I was right and it began to bother me. It took everything in me to tell her she was wrong. To my surprise, she actually admitted to making a mistake.

From that day on, that one experience made me feel comfortable enough to ask questions to find out how she came up with an answer. It also showed the other students that she was not as bad as everyone thought she was and it made a huge difference. That's why it is an old and wise saying, "No one's perfect, everybody makes mistakes." It is nothing wrong with anyone telling you you are wrong or you have made a mistake. It's better for someone to correct your mistakes than for you to go on not knowing your mistake. It never hurts to get help from someone.

Sense of Humor

Sense of Humor – Effective teachers do not take everything so seriously and make learning fun.

- ✓ They have the ability to break the ice in difficult situations with humor.
- ✓ They bring humor into the classroom.
- ✓ They enjoy laughing *with* the class (but, not at the expense of a student).

Learning is serious business, but it can also be fun. Humor is a way of being able to bring joy to an unpleasant task or situation. It is a way of removing tension and "breaking the ice." It allows the teacher to let go of the notion that she always has to be serious and stern-faced when in front of a room full of children.

Humor gives you an effective tool for getting and holding the attention of your students. One of the key benefits of having the characteristic of a Sense of Humor is that it's a great stress reliever—for you as well as for your students. Nothing can break a tense situation better than a corny joke.

Marilyn Mitchell, while teaching at a middle school in Lawrence, Michigan, presented an activity in laughter vs. stress. The exercise involved having the children sit in chairs and hold the edges of the chairs firmly while they tensed every muscle. She then asked students to try to laugh loudly while still tensely gripping their chairs. The students learned that it's next to impossible to hold on to stress while laughing. Laughter means letting go of tension (Girdlefanny, 2005).

You don't have to be a comedian in order to create a humorous learning environment. It is possible to have a serious learning environment while at the same time have a classroom where students are laughing and having fun while they learn. The humor should be spontaneous, comfortable, and appropriate for the situation. The humor should not be at the expense of your students. You should not allow your students to "play the dozens" in your class where they take turns jokingly insulting one another's mother. But, they should be encouraged to share jokes they may have gotten off the internet, in an email or from a joke book that is appropriate for the classroom environment.

I recall once while teaching my college graduate Child Development class, my students were debating whether pre-kindergarten was a good idea. Those students who were opposed to pre-kindergarten argued that teachers were already taking too much of the responsibility that parents should be doing and that a four-year-old should not be forced to be a part of the formally structured learning environment. Those in favor of pre-kindergarten argued that it would be a good idea because children would come to kindergarten ready to learn. The discussion got very heated, and tempers began to flare. I broke the tension by stating, "It is obvious that we have a disagreement on this matter. But can we all just get along!?" The classroom roared with laughter!

I was in a workshop where the presenter was giving some of the grim statistics facing many of the children in the public schools across the country including: increased dropout rates, latch key kids, drugs, teen pregnancy, gangs, single parent homes, etc. As the presenter ended these statistics, there was a bleak look on the faces of those of us in the audience. We were quiet and somber. Then the presenter said, "But, in spite of these grim statistics, I got some good news!" Everyone perked up to hear the good news. She then said, "I just saved a bundle on my car insurance by switching to Geico!" The room erupted with laughter. She then stated, "You guys were looking so sad that I had to say something to cheer you up!" We all laughed again!

I was at E. D. Nixon Elementary, a local elementary school where I tutor math. A little girl was at the board explaining how to do a math problem. She was going at it and pointing to the class explaining the word problem on the board. I got so excited that I said to her, "Go ahead! Girrrrl, you are preaching now! Tell them! Tell them how to do that math problem! Aaaamen!!!" I pulled out a dollar from my wallet and said, "Let me just take up an offering for you!" The class started laughing, and the other students got actively involved in the lesson.

Humor can contribute to the learning atmosphere by increasing attention and motivation by encouraging students to be more inventive and open to new ideas. Students are willing to take risks in the learning process since mistakes are more tolerable in this environment. Humor can help students learn social skills and appropriate societal interactions. It can give a sense of logical perception (Lipman, 2004).

Humor helps to take a student out of her or his normal frame of reference and let the student see that the situation may not be as bad as she or he thinks. With laughter, a student can see the silliness of the situation. It helps students see new possibilities in a perceived complicated situation.

Humor helps students tackle challenging tasks without feeling overwhelmed. Having a classroom environment full of humor, where children can laugh and have fun, makes the learning process enjoyable. Even when teaching a difficult concept, laughter, in the words of Mary Poppins, is like a "spoonful of sugar (that) helps the medicine go down. In a most delightful way!"

"Where We At?"
by
D'Erica Jones

During junior high school, I had a teacher by the name of Ms. Annie Brown. Ms. Brown was the most effective teacher I had because of her sense of humor. Ms. Brown always had us laughing about any little thing. I enjoyed going to her class. Her style and ability to teach were great.

Ms. Brown taught English by using slang. This was a great technique. Ms. Brown would say something like, "Where we at?" then we would correct her by saying, "Where are we?" So, by using this technique we understood more and more how to use correct grammar. Ms. Brown also required us to write our own sentences on the board instead of using a book or doing a worksheet, and if any mistakes were made, she would explain our mistakes to us.

She would pair us into groups and have us grade classmates' papers by making corrections on their papers. Ms. Brown would then come around to see what each student had done and then grade the papers herself. Ms. Brown felt that this way, we could learn from our peers as well as from the instruction she provided.

Ms. Brown was my most effective teacher due to her sense of humor and her unique teaching style that I loved and now use in my own class. Ms. Brown is still teaching and continues to use humor as a part of her teaching style.

Taming of the Shrew
by
Amy M. Crow

My senior year was my most memorable year at Russell County High School. The pep rallies, the football games, and my high school sweetheart. But the thing I remember most is my English teacher, Ms. McTier (she was also the senior advisor). Ms. McTier was about 5'7" with blonde hair, and she was an African American teacher! She looked like she was about 24 years old.

Ms. McTier was a teacher with a sense of humor. She always had a smile on her face. She was always joking with her students. She would start the day with a joke, and her class would be interesting all day long.

I remember when there was death in her family, she came in the classroom and her eyes were red, as if she had been crying, but upon entering the classroom, she began to smile. She remembered the good times she and this family member had together. Most teachers would not be able to go through the day, but Ms. McTier stayed at school that whole day.

She had a great sense of humor, but she was no joke when it came to doing your work. Her classroom was so much fun, but at the same time, there was a lot of work involved. I remember one occasion when we had to read *Taming of the Shrew.* She required us to buy the book so we could read it in class.

Most of the students did not buy the book. Ms. McTier was upset because she made it clear to us that the book was a requirement and when it came time for mid-term, most of us failed.

When we failed mid-term and faced the possibility of not graduating—we knew she meant business. We purchased the book and read it. I appreciate all that she taught me because out of all of my teachers, she inspired me to want to become a teacher. I want to touch a child's life the same way she touched mine.

Never Miss an Opportunity to Laugh
by
Katie Gaston

Sixth grade was one of the most memorable elementary school years. A new school year always bring change, but this one brought change more than ever. I was beginning a new grade, new school, and new friends. I was terrified!

As the first day began, I waited anxiously outside Bear Elementary School. Standing outside in line, according to homeroom, I was pleased to realize the only person I knew at Bear, my best friend, was in my class. All of a sudden my fears were calmed. As we walked inside, our teacher got us seated and the best school year began.

My teacher was Mrs. Lucy Moody. She was the liveliest teacher I had ever seen. Mrs. Moody was fun, loud and of course, serious. Sounds kind of contradictory, but she balanced all her qualities nicely.

Mrs. Moody exemplified many characteristics of an effective teacher. It is hard to choose just one. The characteristic that sticks out the most would be her sense of humor. From day one of sixth grade, it seemed she was always making us laugh. We were having fun and learning all at the same time. This characteristic is the one that "broke the ice" and truly made me excited about my new school.

Throughout the year, Mrs. Moody always laughed and played with us. I felt like I had the coolest teacher. My grades were awesome during the sixth grade. I attribute all of my good grades and bright memories of sixth grade to Mrs. Moody. This was the year I knew I wanted to become a teacher and be just like her.

In my classroom, I see myself acting like she did. I try to be fun, loving and serious while teaching my lessons. We never miss an opportunity to laugh. Knowing now what I know about the paperwork, politics, and behind-the-scenes work involved in the teaching profession, I need to take time to laugh.

I respect Mrs. Moody even more today than during the sixth grade. I will never forget the sixth grade and my awesome teacher, Mrs. Lucy Moody.

The Great Debate
by
Andrea Brown

Living in a world with thousands of teachers and meeting new teachers every year, I only had one favorite. During elementary and middle school, I attended St. Paul Cathedral School. There I met my favorite teacher, Mr. Jones.

Mr. Jones was a very intelligent older black man. He was my eighth grade teacher. He was always filled with humor, everytime we entered his class. We all knew Mr. Jones was a cool teacher, but at the same time, we knew when he meant business. He would joke with us all the time during every lesson. He put fun and laughter into his teaching. As a future teacher, I believe it is very important to have a relationship with your students, at a business level, while keeping them interested in learning.

In Mr. Jones' class we had the same assignment everyday. That assignment was to watch the news every night. Every morning he would go down each row to ask what we saw on the news the night before. That was our class discussion for the morning—what was going on in our world. Every student would get a chance to voice their opinion and if someone disagreed with another person they would hold a debate for five minutes. The remainder of the class was the audience for the debaters. It was up to the audience to decide who won the debate. It was like a game show, and the audience was able to ask questions after the debate.

We all enjoyed the debate game. It made the news more interesting and gave every student an opportunity to talk. The teaching world needs more teachers like Mr. Jones.

Prune Juice Will Fix It!
by
Larrisa Armstead

Elementary school was a fun time for me. I attended the same school from pre-school through sixth grade—Saint John Resurrection Academy. I can still remember each and every one of my teachers, but mostly, Mrs. Rochelle Robbins, my fifth grade teacher.

Mrs. Robbins exuded great personality. She was a short, light skinned, round lady. Every morning, she had to have her coffee and I was always ready, if she chose me, to fill the coffee maker with water for the morning. I was always eager to please.

While Mrs. Robbins had all the qualities of an effective teacher, the one I appreciated the most was her sense of humor. Mrs. Robbins' sense of humor made each day easier. I was always looking forward to what she would say in class. One famous statement will always stick out in my mind.

In elementary school, many children did like to pretend to be sick in order to get out of doing work. A student would sometimes come up to her and mention he had a stomachache, throbbing toe, sore throat, itchy eyes, pain in his writing hand, etc. No matter what problem one had her solution was always the same—prune juice! I can hear her now, "You need some prune juice. That will clear you right up!"

Well, when she would say this, we would laugh because we were elementary students and this would be her solution to every problem under the sun. On some days, she would be serious if she saw a student was really in need of help. But on most days, it was, "Prune juice will fix it!" Our classroom was full of laughter because of her playful yet serious tone. Sometimes a student would act sick just so we could hear her say, "Prune juice will fix it!"

I appreciated this characteristic because I am a very humorous person also. My day does not go well unless I have a sufficient amount of laughter. No one can be serious all day. Mrs. Robbins' sense of humor was also an attention getter and helped to transition into different subjects throughout the day. After all, she taught five out of seven subjects. Therefore, she had to know how to keep our attention for the majority of the day. Mrs. Robbins was an effective teacher and her sense of humor gave her the ultimate edge she needed.

Gives Respect to Students

Gives Respect to Students - Effective teachers do not deliberately embarrass students.

Teachers who give the highest respect, get the highest respect. Examples:

- ✓ Respect students' privacy when returning test papers.
- ✓ Speak to students in private concerning grades or conduct.
- ✓ Effective teachers were remembered for showing sensitivity for students' feelings, and for consistently avoiding situations that might unnecessarily embarrass students.

Students are individuals and each brings something special to the classroom. An effective teacher is one who is able to build upon her students' diverse backgrounds and past experiences and use these differences to create an open and loving classroom. Therefore, it is important that you respect each student's multicultural history and incorporate those values into your classroom. In order for a classroom to be a flourishing learning environment, the most important ingredient is respect.

In order for a student to comprehend the material presented, he or she must be in a welcoming environment. If students are going to be successful learners, they need to feel respected by their peers and especially by their teacher.

Under the ideal situation, respect is a two-way-street—the teacher respects students and students respect the teacher. However, in reality, this is not always the case. But in spite of this, you must always respect your students, even when they don't respect you! I know at times this may be hard, but it is vital if you are going to reach your most difficult students. Also, you must create a classroom environment where students respect each other.

When a student steps over the line by not treating you or a peer with proper respect, (and sooner or later, it will happen) the atmosphere of the classroom will become disrupted and the learning environment will suffer. Students will be deprived of instructional time and will not be able to concentrate on the task at hand. Therefore, when an incident occurs, it is critical that you quickly respond in a manner that will encourage respect in the future.

Your classroom rules should focus on respect as the essential part of a healthy learning atmosphere. Having students to sign a behavior contract at the beginning of the school year is one good way to ensure students abide by the guidelines established in your classroom.

You should create a classroom that has a sense of community where each student has something to add and where it is okay to respectfully disagree (Ritzer & Sleigh, 2001). You should allow students an opportunity to give their input in the creation of class rules.

When a disruption does occur, strive to see an issue from the student's perspective. Ask the student for ideas on how to better the situation in the future. Such as, "Angelina, what do you think would be a better way to handle your disagreement with Stella in the future?"

It goes without saying that students will make mistakes. And from time to time, rules will be broken. But as the teacher, you must be patient and have consistency in managing your classroom. Student-teacher interactions must be based on mutual respect; without it, classroom management will be a major problem, and a positive learning environment will be almost impossible to achieve (Court T.V., 2005).

The R.E.S.P.E.C.T Pledge!
by
Tameka Sanders

"R.E.S.P.E.C.T! FIND OUT WHAT IT MEANS TO ME!" I will never forget that song for as long as I live. It has played over and over in my head for many years. I will never forget the very first time I understood what it meant to give, show, and learn respect for myself as well as others. Mrs. Hardy, my third grade teacher, made sure that we knew the meaning of respect. Everyday we had to enter the classroom and repeat a pledge that was taped to our desktop that helped us remember to respect each other as well as ourselves. The pledge stated:

"I pledge to respect my classmates as well as myself. I will not disrespect my classmates or my teacher and I will be sure to respect older people. I pledge to respect myself and to remember that respect will take me a long way as long as I remember to give it. I will always remember that I must give respect to get respect."

Mrs. Hardy was like a mother away from home. She would always stress the importance of respect. If students in her class acted out or didn't show respect for each other, she would make us recite the pledge attached to our desktop. I would never forget when I wanted to be the "class clown." Mrs. Hardy made me apologize to the entire class and recite the pledge.

Mrs. Hardy was one of those teachers who believed that respect was a must and without it, you couldn't grow to love yourself or the people around you. I will always admire Mrs. Hardy for the time and effort she put into stressing the importance of respect. Because of the great impact that Mrs. Hardy has had on my life, I have grown to be respectful in everything that I do.

I have always tried my best to respect others just as I would want them to respect me. I have realized that respect can determine your altitude in life. Respect is also something that must be earned, and without respect you have nothing. "Teach a child what to think and you make him a slave to your knowledge. Teach a child how to think and you make all knowledge his slave." I strongly agree with this quote because this is the exact method that Mrs. Hardy used when she stressed the importance of respect to her students, and I will always remember to do the same for my future students.

Cooking Collard Greens
by
Jackie A. Wyche

Thump! Thump! Thump! We heard his footsteps coming closer, and then they stopped by the teacher's desk. "Good morning class." he said, and our hearts relaxed and started beating normally again. It was the beginning of a new school-year and the most wonderful teacher, Mr. Jones, greeted us. Mr. Jones, my third grade teacher, in St. Petersburg, Florida, at Campbell Park Elementary always came in with a smile on his face and treated everyone fair and as equals.

Mr. Jones had diabetes, so he always carried a brown paper sack full of candies with him. If by chance we were good or we answered a question correctly, we were rewarded with a small but filling piece of candy.

Mr. Jones also liked hands-on activities. Thus, we planted a garden and grew vegetables throughout the year. At least once a week we took a break from sitting in our seats and instead went to water the plants and talked of how they grew and matured so that we could enjoy them later on. Towards the end of the year, we cooked collard greens from our garden and ate them during class. He also let anyone who wanted a plant take one home.

Anyone who didn't know this teacher might think that we had it easy and we were spoiled, but it wasn't like that. Consequently, I am now an eighth grade teacher in a middle school. As I look back on my years in elementary school, Mr. Jones has greatly influenced me to become an educator. In all my years of schooling, I have not met a teacher or another human being as relaxed as he was and who respected me as much as he did.

I have had some people, very few, who have come close. But none of whom have taken his place. Yes, we were only in third grade. But he made us feel good about ourselves and let us know that we could do anything.

Sad to say, Mr. Jones passed away a few years ago as a result of complications from his diabetes. But his legacy still lives among many of his students. He wasn't just some person who did not know what was going on; he was like a father-figure, whom I greatly admired.

Multiplication Mountaineers
by
Stayce Montgomery

What does it mean to be an effective teacher? Effective in the Webster's Dictionary is defined as: having an intended or expected effect; producing a strong impression or response; prepared for use or action; impressive; producing the intended results.

This definition is a perfect description of my most effective teacher. I attended James H. Brown Elementary School in Jonesboro, Georgia. My fourth grade teacher was Mrs. Martha Smith. She was short in stature and had one of the sweetest spirits I had ever seen in my life. She was so genuine and caring. How could one individual have so much character, so much knowledge, so efficient, so much creativity, and so much joy!

Her teaching strategies were straightforward and understandable. She would always have hands-on examples that would incorporate the entire class and leave an everlasting understanding of the subject. Mrs. Smith always found kind and encouraging words to praise individuals as well as good group behavior.

I can personally say that as I become an educator, my everyday goal is to strive to become that effective teacher as Mrs. Smith was unto me—so compassionate, creative and knowledgeable of the subject matter.

I would say what most defined her effectiveness was giving respect to all her students. I can remember Mrs. Smith playing a game with the entire class. We all knew that while playing games, educational or physical, sometimes many would show bad sportsmanship if they were losing. But on this particular day, we were playing multiplication mountaineers, and this game was built around seeing who knew the most multiplication facts.

Well, one little boy became furious because he was losing. He went to another student's desk, threaten to start a fight. Mrs. Smith stopped the game to educate us on sportsmanship and how to respect others. I vaguely remember a time that Mrs. Smith had to deal with major behavior problems from students because she always related well to our everyday needs and wants. She always gave us respect, and in the end, received the same in return.

All-in-all, to be effective in someone's life, you must first understand that as an educator, someone is always looking to you for a little attention, a little compassion, and a little sincerity.

As a prospective teacher, I am making it a personal goal and mission to be that one individual that will never be forgotten, that one individual that will positively change a child's life forever. I want to be that one individual that will be effective. I will leave a positive effect on a child's life like Mrs. Smith left on my life.

The Bone Crusher
by
John Cleckler

In 1974, I enjoyed being a student of Mr. Wells, our 4th grade science teacher. Mr. Wells and his wife were the first African Americans to teach at my rural area school of Verbena, Alabama. I have very fond memories of Mr. Wells, and anytime you bring his name up around my old friends from school, everyone has a story to tell. Mr. Wells was always positive. I cannot see how anyone can have a positive attitude all the time; it takes special people to always see the good in every situation. He was available to his students anytime he was needed. He found ways to reach all students no matter what race or social economic background one might have.

Mr. Wells seemed to enjoy his subject very much. He seemed excited and passionate about everything that related to science. You could tell he really wanted us to learn and understand what he was teaching.

He prepared neat little experiments for us to conduct and always related them to real life situations. He would give us "Life Lessons" talks. I still remember his speeches on smoking, drinking, eating healthy, and many other important things to make our lives better.

Mr. Wells respected students and did not embarrass them in front of the class. I remember many occasions when he would call a student to the back of the room out of view of the rest of the class and talk to the student. I would always wonder why until I found out for myself. I was not paying attention and was goofing off a little when he called me to the back of the class. He got my attention and let me know it would be better for me to get busy doing my work.

I believe Mr. Wells expected all of his students to do well. He would give advice all the time as though we were grown-ups. Mr. Wells was one of the few teachers who took our class on a field trip. We went all the way to Huntsville, Alabama, to visit the NASA Space Program. I could not believe the size of those rockets—they were huge! We all had a great day.

I do not know if Mr. Wells could make it in the educational environment we have today. He was a wonderful man who played innocently with children and had the opportunity to influence many lives. He would wrestle almost everyday with the boys. You would have to be careful when walking by him because he might put a "Charlie Horse" on your leg or put a "Bone Crushing" grip on your ribs. All these things were done as a playful gesture.

I remember Mr. Wells because he seemed as though he really wanted to be there and take care of us. I was a student of Mr. Wells and he loved me—this I know!

Forgiving

Forgiving – Effective teachers do not hold grudges against their students.

- ✓ They are willing to forgive students for inappropriate behavior.
- ✓ They have a habit of starting each day with a clean slate.
- ✓ They understand that an attitude of forgiveness is essential if difficult students are to be reached.
- ✓ They understand that disruptive or antisocial behavior can be upsetting, and quickly turn a teacher against a student, but the willingness to never give up on a difficult student can result in a wonderful success story.

It has been said that, "forgiveness can be good for your health" (Wright, 2008 p.1). But when it comes to forgiving others, it is not always an easy thing to do. At some point in time, you may have asked yourself, "Why should I be the one to forgive this member of my family who hurt me, or this principal who ignored my clearly great ideas, or this co-worker who stabbed me in the back, or even this student that frequently misbehaves in my classroom?"

In dealing with students, perhaps you have said to yourself, "Why should I forgive this student? He is going to just do it again! I will forgive him when he changes, or when he asks me to forgive him, or if he stops acting a fool!"

Let face it, regardless of the grade-level, at times students will do and say things that will really make you angry. At times, they are going to get on your last nerve (you know I'm telling the truth)! Based on what the student may have said or done to you, your anger could be perfectly justified.

When someone wrongs you, even a student, your natural reaction is to get even, or to seek revenge. Your anger can be overpowering as you prepare to defend your honor and your career. But, you must stop and realize—they are just children. You are the adult.

Forgiveness is more for you than it is for the person who has wronged you. They may not be hurt or offended in the least by what they did to you. You are the one who wants to be free mentally and emotionally from the hurt. That's why you must forgive. Only you can change how you feel about a situation. You may not be able to control what a student does to you, but you can control how you react and respond to what he or she did. You can choose not to forgive and hold in the resentment, or you can forgive and let go of the hurt.

Forgiveness doesn't mean that you allow yourself to be a 'doormat' for people to walk on. It doesn't mean that you continue to allow yourself to remain in a situation where you are mistreated or abused. If you allow a relative to borrow your car and she wrecks it, you can forgive that relative, but once you get your car repaired, forgiveness doesn't mean that you have to let that relative use your car again.

If a student is extremely disruptive in your classroom, for the sake of the other students, who are being deprived of instructional time, for your own sake, and even for the sake of the student who is being disruptive—you may need to remove that student from your class. But, you should not hold a grudge. You should forgive the student (Wright, 2000).

Forgiveness goes beyond just saying to someone, "I forgive you." Forgiveness is a matter of the heart.

According to psychologist, Dr. Tim Sams, "Forgiveness is a critical element in becoming self-actualized and fully loving. Forgiving is the process by which you let go of feeling victimized or having wronged others. It allows you to climb out of the dark well of anger, bitterness, or guilt into which you can easily fall" (Sams, 2004 p.1).

In order to forgive a student, you must focus on the behavior, not the outcome. What is going on in the student's life that is causing him or her to act this way? When dealing with a student, your acts of forgiveness may result in an immediate change in the student's behavior. As the student gets older, he can look back and realize the great love you showed him in an extremely difficult situation. Also, other students in your class will learn from watching how you respond to this disruptive student. When you develop the characteristic of forgiveness, you are the one who will be set free and receive the blessing (Wiedenhoff, 2004).

The 'N' Word
by
Clayton Hutsler

It was the beginning of integration. The year was 1971. I attended Montgomery Elementary School in Atlanta, Georgia, Dekalb County School District. Mr. Wynn was my 6th grade math teacher. He was the first male teacher who ever taught me. He was also my first black teacher and the first black teacher in my school. Mr. Wynn was in his early thirties, had a mustache and a short afro. He reminded me of Bill Cosby or the teacher on the then popular television show, *Room 222*.

Mr. Wynn didn't have a favorite student, and he treated us all special. His teaching style was to start with a tiny simple idea, and then move to more complicated concepts, so the hard material seemed simple. He made everything seem interesting, and all the students loved his class. He would have discussions about all sorts of things going on in the world, the community, and in our class. It seemed we would talk every afternoon about one thing or another. Everyone in the class participated, and no one was ever made to feel stupid or ashamed about what they thought. One time he gave the class a lesson on how to brush your teeth, and described the process in a way that those students who did brush regularly and those who did not all learned something.

The most vivid memory I have of Mr. Wynn's class is the time Joey Knight was rocking his chair during an instructional movie film (The old reel-to-reel type. This was before the days of VCR and DVD). Mr. Wynn walked up to Joey's chair and quickly pushed it to the floor. Joey was startled, and shouted, "Damn, nigger!" The class all focused their attention on Joey and Mr. Wynn. Mr. Wynn looked Joey in the eyes, and told him to go out in the hall. He went next door to Mrs. Walker's class and pulled her out of her classroom. He and Mrs. Walker took Joey to the principal's office. Mr. Wynn kept his cool in front of the class, and showed us that he would never lose his control, and we would be safe around him. When Mr. Wynn returned to his class, he carried on as he normally did. Joey was suspended for his comment and when he returned, Mr. Wynn treated him no different than any other student.

Stealing a Snack
by
Courtney Giles

The most effective teacher that I had while attending grammar school was my 3rd grade teacher, Mrs. Virginia Ozment, at Livingston Jr. High School. My third grade class was self-contained. If I had to choose one effective teacher characteristic to describe Mrs. Ozment, I would most definitely have to say that Mrs. Ozment was very forgiving. The students always felt as if they could go to her to discuss any issue.

For example, one day I forgot my snack money and didn't bring anything to eat. One of my classmates left her snack on her desk and I quickly took it, put it in my pocket, and asked to go to the restroom. Instead of going to the restroom, I went outside and ate the snack.

When I returned and snack time had arrived, I felt really bad to see Latawna crying—the girl whose snack I had taken. Mrs. Ozment and Latawna searched everywhere. Another classmate shared his snack with her. The next morning I admitted to Mrs. Ozment that I had stolen and eaten Latawna's snack. She told me how disappointed she was to know that it was her best student ever who had done such a thing. She also told me that I was still a wonderful person by admitting that I had done wrong and that I should apologize to Latawna and bring her a snack the next day. Mrs. Ozment continued to treat me nice. I really felt as if I could trust Mrs. Ozment and I still do. However, Latawna had a more difficult time forgiving me.

Making a Preacher Go Bad
by
Sharmaine Goldsmith

The most effective teacher that I have had the pleasure of learning from was Mrs. Dorothy Whelchel. She was a 6th grade teacher. She taught all the academic subjects. Mrs. Whelchel was a Christian woman. She often said that our class would "make a preacher go bad." Although she encountered behavioral problems daily, she was always forgiving of those who tried to make her job more difficult than it already was. Her willingness to easily forgive is why she is my most effective teacher.

One day while Mrs. Whelchel was teaching a math lesson, one of her most troubling students, TaCory Washington, threw a balled up sheet of paper at her head. She turned around and asked who threw the paper. No one responded. Another student then pointed to TaCory and told her that he had thrown the paper. Now, TaCory had been in trouble all day for throwing food in the lunchroom and for cursing another student. This was the last straw for Mrs. Whelchel. Because TaCory was on his last strike, she wrote him up and sent him to the office where he remained the rest of the day.

The next day, Mrs. Whelchel began the day as always. She greeted us all at the door, including TaCory. He seemed shocked that she was so nice to him after what he had done the previous day. That afternoon, he apologized to her and she accepted. After that day, Mrs. Whelchel no longer had problems with TaCory Washington, and he went on to pass the 6th grade.

Her forgiving TaCory has always been in my memory. I know that it was hard for her to do because he hit her with a ball of paper. She inspired me that day.

Boys Will Be Boys
by
Darrell A. Morgan

Teachers endure a lot of abuse and, as a student, I was no different when it came to issuing the abuse. It is really nice when there is a teacher who is willing to forgive and move on.

I attended Peterson Elementary School. It was the year I was in the third grade. My third grade teacher was Mrs. Burke. She was, in my opinion, a great teacher, and also a very pretty teacher. I had a crush on her. I did something wrong one day (boys will be boys) and she chastised me. She grabbed my arm and marched me down to the principal's office. She wrote me a referral, and a note was sent home to my parents. I was in trouble, so I had to think of some way to get out of this trouble I had gotten myself into. So, I lied and said she slapped me. My father and mother were furious, and this started a series of events that ended in Mrs. Burke going through a lot of unnecessary heartache and pain—as a result of my lie.

She talked to me and my parents along with the principal of Peterson Elementary. In this meeting, I stuck to my story that she had slapped me. I was asked a series of questions by everyone in the room, but I stuck to my story. This lady was in trouble and had done nothing wrong. The meeting ended with me standing outside the room. I don't know what was said, but Mrs. Burke came out crying, and I felt really bad.

The next day I went to class, and Mrs. Burke did not treat me any different. I told my parents that I had lied—that I thought she was very pretty and I did something to her that I should not have done.

We had another meeting. In the meeting, I started crying and apologized to Mrs. Burke. Thanks to Mrs. Burke's willingness to forgive me, we were able to put an end to this ugly situation that I had created.

The Worst Class Ever
by
AlFreda J. Brown

Third grade at Westhills Elementary was a year to remember. I can remember it like it was yesterday. I was greeted with a smile from a woman by the name of Rhonda Wesley. Mrs. Wesley introduced herself as my third grade teacher and I can remember feeling a sigh of relief. Mrs. Wesley was the most forgiving teacher that I have ever encountered in my school career. I am sure my third grade class was one of her most challenging years of teaching. My class was labeled the worst class that had ever attended Westhills Elementary.

Mrs. Wesley would forgive you for anything that happened in or outside her classroom. For example, when we received a surprise visit from the board of education, my classmates decided to pull the fire alarm. It was pouring rain outside; we were all outside for about 30 minutes which felt like eternity.

I clearly remember the look of hurt and embarrassment on Mrs. Wesley's face. She led us back into the classroom and asked us to gather on her big round, bright carpet. I recall her saying, "Each day we start with a clean slate and this, too, shall pass." She began to read a short story to us. I do not remember what the story was about, but I do remember the book having large pictures and words. We were then told to go back to our seats and write a paragraph about the importance of fire and safety at school. I remember thinking to myself, "What does this have to do with the book she just read to us?" Little did I know, Mrs. Wesley read because she needed to relieve some stress.

My classmates and I went back to our seats and began to write. After all 20 of us shared our essays, she began to explain to us why we should never attempt to pull the fire alarm again. We all expected Mrs. Wesley to be angry at us for months, but she was not.

Two months later our class was on the right track, completing homework assignments and receiving complements from other teachers. Mrs. Wesley decided that she would reward us for our good behavior. One Friday afternoon, we were told that we would be getting a treat. Mrs. Wesley asked that we place our heads on our desks. She was going to the freezer to get some ice cream, and if we were quiet, we would have free time on the playground. I was so excited, ice cream and free play instead of taking a math test!

When Mrs. Wesley left the classroom, we were all silent. Then all of a sudden, I felt a kick in my back. It was Darren kicking me! I had had enough and it was time to react. I began beating him against the wall. Another third grade teacher, Mrs. Cox, ran into the room and removed me from Darren. However, it was too late. The damage was already done. Blood was everywhere. Darrin had to be sent to the emergency room for stitches.

One part of me had a sense of relief because I knew that he would never pick on me again, and the other part of me felt a sense of disappointment because I knew that Mrs. Wesley would be disappointed. However, that afternoon about six o'clock, the doorbell rang and it was Mrs. Wesley. She was at my house. She spoke with both my parents about Darren's stitches and assured them that he would have a rapid recovery. My mom was grateful to hear the news. I apologized to Mrs. Wesley for what had happened and she once again assured me that I was forgiven, and sometimes a little girl has to do what a little girl has to do. Darrin and I both talked with our parents present and became the best of friends throughout our school career.

I knew after these two major incidents that Mrs. Wesley was a forgiving teacher who started each day with a clean slate no matter what happened the day before. My third grade year was my best year of elementary school. I am grateful for having had Mrs. Wesley and I try my best to start each day in my own classroom with a clean slate.

I Love Lucy
by
Shecarie Wilkerson

My favorite teacher throughout my entire high school years was Mrs. Lambert. She was my tenth grade Algebra teacher at Linden High School. Mrs. Lambert was my favorite teacher because she was one of the kindest, most caring and considerate people that I've ever met. She would always put the students first. Mrs. Lambert displayed several of the 12 Characteristics of an Effective Teacher, but the one she displayed most was "forgiving." I say this because there was this one student that we considered the biggest class clown. Well, one day Mrs. Lambert stepped outside of the classroom, the student peeped in the role book and noticed Mrs. Lambert first name, which was Lucille.

When Mrs. Lambert came back in the classroom, the student yelled out and called her Lucille Ball (*I Love Lucy* T.V. character), and the whole class began to laugh. I could tell that Mrs. Lambert was more hurt than angry by looking at the expression on her face. Her whole face turned red and she sent the student to the office.

Despite this, Mrs. Lambert didn't treat the student any different from the rest of the class. At the end of the school year, she awarded him with a good behavior certificate. She also hugged that student's neck and told him that she would miss him being in her class. In other words, this was Mrs. Lambert's way of saying, "I forgive you for all the trouble you put me through this year!"

He Spit in Her Face!
by
Tiffany Persons

Many teachers have various characteristics of an effective teacher. As I thought about the characteristics of an effective teacher, I thought about my second grade teacher, Mrs. McNair. Mrs. McNair was a very amiable person. She always kept a beautiful smile on her face no matter what. You could never tell when she was mad or if she just wanted to walk out of the class and never come back.

Mrs. McNair possessed many of the characteristics of an effective teacher. The characteristic that stood out the most was that she was very forgiving. There was this incident that happened in our second grade class. We were taking our usual spelling test on Friday. After we finished our test, Mrs. McNair would assign us seatwork until she finished grading our tests. She would give them back as soon as she was finished grading them.

There was a boy in our class who failed every test. After a couple of spelling tests, I guess he was tired of making bad grades. When he received his test, he started screaming very loud. Mrs. McNair ran to him and asked what was wrong. He started to throw things and became out of control. She was trying to calm him down and all of a sudden, he spit in her face. Then he got out of his desk and kicked her as hard as he could. Mrs. McNair finally gained control of him. She took him outside and talked to him. I never heard her raise her voice. For the rest of the day and the school year, Mrs. McNair did not treat the boy any different. You could not tell if she was mad at him that day; even if she was, she did not show it. That day she continued to smile as usual. She did not look at him strange or anything.

I did not understand why she did not show her anger or why she continued to treat him nice. I understand now because I have been in that situation. I learned that you cannot show that you are mad or treat a child different because of what they have done. You must handle the situation like a professional at all times.

Too Many Beers
by
Duran Odoms

During the fall of my senior year in high school, I had an unfortunate incident to take place. I had gone home after school to get ready for a game during football season and while I was there, I consumed two beers from a friend of mine. The band director found out about this incident from other students and I was kicked out of the band.

Mrs. Keefer was my Physics teacher and had taught me previously when I was in tenth and eleventh grade. I was the representative for the Senior Class of the Student Government Association of Monroe County High School. We were getting ready to attend the state convention and only officers in good standing could attend the convention. She always told us the truth and looked beneath our troubles.

When spring came and it was time for the state convention, our treasurer had gotten pregnant and there had to be a replacement for her. Mrs. Keefer made the decision to appoint me as the treasurer and allowed me to go the state convention. Forgiveness must be a trait that all teachers and administrators possess, because students will always make mistakes and will need to receive help from someone.

Losing My Bad Attitude
by
Keri Crosby

When I was in the sixth grade, my favorite teacher was my math teacher. Her name was Ms. Angie Wilson. I was the type of child who worked only when the teacher would be watching or in the room. I started having trouble with fractions and asked questions. Ms. Wilson did help me but then she had to help other students—I wanted more attention. Ms. Wilson continued to work with the other students, and I lost my cool. I got smart with her and then she heard me being rude and disrespectful. Ms. Wilson called my parents, and my father had a long talk with me.

Normally, I would have received a whipping for my misbehavior. Well, my father told me to apologize and to stop acting up. The next day, I apologized, even though I still had an attitude. When Ms. Wilson asked if I needed any help, I would lie and say no—knowing that I really needed help. I chose to let my grade drop and keep the bad attitude.

Ms. Wilson continued to check on me even when I told her that I did not need any help. Finally, one day she called me out in the hallway to speak with me about my failing grades. She informed me that I was the cause of my grades and that she was concerned. She also told me that she was here for me and that she would do all she could to help me so that I could bring my grades back up. So I lost the attitude and I started making 'A's and 'B's, and Ms. Wilson kept her word that she would help me.

Breaking the Overhead Projector
by
Tamara Mitchell

Mrs. Novak, my fifth grade teacher, was a person who would not hold grudges against her students. I remember being in a situation that was very hard to forgive. I was chasing a student in the classroom. The student tripped on the overhead projector, and it broke.

When Mrs. Novak asked what happened, the student explained that I was chasing him and that's how he tripped and knocked over the projector. Mrs. Novak never showed her anger, but we knew that she was disappointed with us. Mrs. Novak made sure we both received equal and fair punishment. When the student and I returned from our punishment, Mrs. Novak never treated us differently.

Double Jeopardy
by
Andrea Steele

Everyone has his or her memories of their time in high school. Some may remember it as time served or time wasted. Others might describe it as the best of times, and others, the worst of times. I choose to reflect on my four years in high school as the height of my learning experience.

During my time in high school, I had the pleasure of interacting with quite a few teachers, principals, and librarians. Needless to say, I was the one you wanted to look out for. I wasn't what one would call a troubled child. I was more of the child who liked to find trouble. My junior year, I would skip class and go home to watch Jerry Springer or music videos on BET, not because I was addicted to it, but because I noticed that my teacher didn't seem to notice when I wasn't in class. We seldom had to turn work in at the end of class. My teacher, Mr. Ray, took up everything at the beginning. So it was prefect. I stayed a few streets away from the school and had a little car—so I was home in five minutes.

This lasted about three weeks before I was ratted out. Mr. Ray was furious and had me suspended for two weeks. I was angry at the informant more than anything else. Well, when I came back from my school-ordered vacation, all of my teachers treated me different. It lasted for a while. All my teachers except one lady named Mrs. Sims. She told me that she wasn't going to label me as a problem child or as a child who could not be trusted. I was going to have to prove to her that I was a problem child with my actions, and if she didn't see it then it didn't happen in her eyes. I appreciated her views on it and actually she became my favorite teacher.

I think that exemplifies the quality of an effective teacher—forgiveness! I had already been punished for my wrongdoings and she didn't give me the double jeopardy that the other teachers did by losing trust in me and labeling me as a bad child. When Mrs. Sims gave me a chance, I proved to her that I was not only a good person but I was smart and trustworthy. My junior and senior years went a lot smoother. I received great grades—nothing but 'A's and 'B's. I stayed at school the whole day (most days). I owe that turnaround in my academic focus to my teacher Mrs. Sims for her display of effectiveness in forgiveness as a teacher.

Compassionate

Compassionate - Effective teachers are genuinely concerned about students' personal problems and can relate to them.

✓ The teacher takes a special interest in helping students solve personal problems.
✓ Students can tell that their teacher loves them.
✓ The sensitivity and compassion of a caring teacher affects students in profound and lasting ways.

Compassion was the one characteristic students wrote and spoke about most often. Students who wrote about the teacher who showed them compassion shared some of the most personal, emotional, and heartwarming stories. Even when they were describing another dominant characteristic of their favorite teacher, the word compassion would be used in the description. Students submitted so many essays on compassion that it was difficult to select those to be included in this book. As you read these essays, you may, as I did, get a little teary eyed. Therefore, having some tissue nearby would be a good idea.

***

There is a familiar saying that, "Children won't care how much you know until they know how much you care." In other words, children are more influenced by how much a teacher cares about them than how much the teacher knows the subject being taught. Think about it, when was the last time you heard a child say, "My teacher is really smart" compared to "My teacher is really nice!" When a child says, "My teacher is really nice!" she is *really* saying, "My teacher loves me!"

When you analyze the truly effective teachers, you will also find lovable, caring, warm people. Effective teachers know that they cannot get students to learn unless students know the teacher cares about them. Ineffective teachers think that all they have to do is teach the subject matter and that will be enough. "I was hired to teach. I was not hired to deal with these kids personal issues!" An effective teacher knows that unless you deal with students' personal problems, you will never be able to teach them the subject matter.

To truly care for the children in your classroom requires no money, it is not something that you go to an in-service workshop to learn, and you are definitely not going to learn it in you college courses—it comes from the heart.

The most sincere form of service comes from listening, caring, and loving. In the words of Harry K. Wong, author of the best selling book, *The First Days of School,* "You don't need to tell a class that you love them, but you certainly can show it. If you choose to be a significant and effective person in a student's life, you must demonstrate your care and love both implicitly through your body language and explicitly through what you say" (Wong, 2001 p. 76).

To be compassionate means considering the needs of your students before your own needs. Putting your students' needs before your own sometimes is hard (Raatma, 2000). But, when you are in the classroom, your students should be your first priority. You will be astonished at the kind of impact you have on your students!

The teacher must be excited and compassionate because students learn best when they are in the classroom of a caring teacher. Many students are not intrinsically motivated. They need some type of outside source to encourage them to do the class assignments and learn the material. If they know that their teacher truly cares about them, they will do their work and behave appropriately to please the teacher. This fact is true regardless of the grade-level of the student.

You may have heard some of the philosophical statements about being a teacher, such as: "Teaching is more a ministry than a profession." "Teaching is a calling." "Teachers are born, not made." Whether you believe these statements or not, as you read these essays on compassion, you may gain a better understanding as to why such statements about teaching exist, and why having compassion is so vital if you wish to become an effective teacher.

Beautiful Inside and Out
by
Mary E. Williams

Educators must have a true and sincere love for children to be effective. There are 12 characteristics of an effective teacher, but the one characteristic I perceive to be the most important is Compassion.

I attended Mac Davis Elementary School in Montgomery, Alabama. I was 11 years old when my 5th grade teacher, Mrs. Mice Hill Wright, showed me just how a teacher can have a profound effect on students. I am from a very large family of 10 children, and I am the fifth child of the 10. My best friend Debra was from a small family with only two children. She had very nice clothes, long hair, and everyone thought she was very pretty, even me. I, on the other hand; had very short hair, hand-me-down clothes, but always clean. Although I wasn't as fortunate as she, I never thought of myself as ugly or less fortunate.

One day I overheard a teacher ask Debra, "Why do you always hang with Mary? She is so ugly!" That statement crushed me. I never told my parents, I just kept it to myself. Mrs. Wright noticed a change in me. She kept me in one day from recess and asked me if I had a problem that I wanted to talk about. She told me that I didn't have that happy smile that she had grown to love.

I started to cry, and she held me. I told her what I overheard this teacher say to Debra about me. She said to me, "Dry your eyes," as she took her hand and lifted my face. Mrs. Wright never had children of her own, she said, "You are beautiful both inside and out. If I had a little girl, I would want her to look just like you."

I knew then that I wanted to be a teacher. Mrs. Wright showed me the true meaning of what it feels like to be shown compassion. One teacher lowered my self-esteem, but another motivated me to the point where I never let another person define what I thought of myself. A profound and lasting effect is what Mrs. Wright's compassion left on me, leaving me still to this day with the lasting impression that, "I am Mary, and I am beautiful inside and out." Thank you, Mrs. Wright, for showing a shattered happy-go-lucky poor girl like me compassion and love that I will never forget.

Special "Monica Assignments"
by
Monica McKinney

Becoming a teacher takes a little heart and a strong knowledge base, but becoming an effective one takes a lifetime of experience and intrinsic qualities that serve as guides for instruction. The qualities effective teachers possess enable them to make grand impacts on their students, both academically and personally.

During my third grade year of school at Simpson Elementary in Franklin, Kentucky, I encountered a true gem of a teacher, Mrs. Betty Brown, whose compassionate spirit helped me work through a very difficult time in my life.

When I was eight-years-old, my mother was killed in a drunk-driving accident, and I was left with many perplexing questions about life and death. Not until I entered Mrs. Brown's classroom did I encounter someone who wished to help me deal with the issues ushered in by my mother's untimely death.

The first day of class, Mrs. Brown had a special conference with me, and we began to discuss my feelings about what had transpired within the past few months of my life. She gave me special, "Monica Assignments" that enabled me to explore reading material that focused on grief therapy for young children.

Many of the literary works were children's books that told of stories about pets and close friends and relatives that had passed. These activities helped me to grieve my mother's death and bring some understanding, from a child's perspective, to my mother's passing. Aside from aiding me in working through my mother's death, Mrs. Brown showed her compassionate spirit by going the extra mile with students from underprivileged homes, students with academic or behavior issues, and students with low self-esteem and self-respect. She made it her number one priority to ensure that everyone felt special and received all the necessary attention and guidance needed to enhance the learning experience.

A major goal of my life is to become an educator who embodies Mrs. Brown's compassionate heart. Her selfless and sincere attempts to ease my transition into life without my mother were truly the greatest gifts anyone could have given me. The time she spent working with me after school and during her planning was not something just any teacher would have done, but was an approach of a truly effective teacher. By helping me deal with those newfound issues, I felt important to her, thus important to her classroom and the learning experience. By introducing me to material that was relevant to my situation, she ultimately worked to ensure that my learning and personal development would be of paramount importance.

Not the End of the World
by
Lakeisha Parrish

The most effective teacher that had the most impact on my life as a student and as a person was my high school basketball coach. Coach Larry Geoghagen taught health and physical education at Walton Senior High School in DeFuniak Springs, Florida. Being compassionate was the characteristic that stood out the most and made him an effective teacher.

The women's basketball team had just come off a Final Four appearance in the 4A state championship tournament. With everyone coming back, the future looked bright. Our team was also slated to represent the state of Florida in a national tournament that would be held in Ogden, Utah. Before we could participate in the tournament everyone had to have an athletic physical. During the physical it was discovered that I was pregnant.

The first thing I thought was that my mother was going to kill me. I was so scared and ashamed that it literally made me sick. The first person I confided in was Coach Geoghagen. The first thing he did was hugged my neck and explained to me that this was not the end of the world. He reassured me that he would be there for me and the only thing I should be worried about was telling my family and taking care of myself. He also accompanied me when I told my mother. This kind of compassion is why I worked harder than anyone because I knew that whatever the situation may be, he believed in me and had my back. He also made me realize that nothing in life is easy and going to school, playing basketball, and having a baby would only test my will to succeed.

Deodorant Soap
by
Terry Edmonds

My favorite teacher was Mrs. Lewis. I was in her fifth grade class at Ernie Pyle Elementary School in Gary, Indiana. She was a very good teacher who made learning fun. She was always prepared and came into the classroom with a positive attitude. I rarely saw her in a bad mood unless one of the students acted up in class, which was not a common thing. She had high expectations for everyone in the class; we were all expected to excel and she would not accept anything but your best.

She was also a compassionate teacher who recognized that not all of her students came from the same economical environment. I remember one day in class she mentioned that there may be some students who did not have deodorant, and that we were older now and should begin using it. She told the class to, "take a bar of soap and rub it under your arm and this could substitute for deodorant." I realize now looking back that she did not want to single anyone out.

Motherly Touch
by
Arnetta Moore

My favorite teacher was Mrs. Jaggers, my third grade math teacher at Court Elementary in Detroit, Michigan. There were 27 students in my class. There was a little boy in my class named William; he always appeared to be sad. He rarely smiled, and had an offensive smell. He also wore dirty clothes. He was the kind of boy who no one would play with.

As I reflect back on my childhood years, in Mrs. Jaggers' class, I think about this one occasion when William did not have on the proper attire for winter in Detroit. Instead of sending William home, Mrs. Jaggers caressed him with her warm motherly embrace, and went into her desk draw and provided William with clean socks, underclothing and gloves. After seeing this act of kindness, I too began to treat him with respect and as a friend.

Mrs. Jaggers did several other kind acts for children. She would put her compassionate personal and motherly touch to every lesson and every student's life. To this day, I keep in contact with Mrs. Jaggers. She is a great leader and a professional role model. As a first year teacher, I strive to be just like Mrs. Jaggers.

My Backbone
by
Chandra L. Barton

There is only one teacher that has stood out over the years. His name is Mr. Lovell Jenkins. Mr. Jenkins was my tenth grade geometry teacher at Jefferson Davis High School.

Mr. Jenkins was the kind of person who joked all the time and loved to call you out. His sense of humor was wonderful because it made me feel more comfortable in the class. I was a jokester myself. One day the joke went too far, and he didn't like it. I joked about his bald head. I apologized, and he forgave me.

Mr. Jenkins had compassion and the passion to teach; especially math. I hated math all through grade school, because teachers didn't take the time to make sure that I had the concepts and applications for doing math. I especially hated word problems. Mr. Jenkins helped me to understand, and even grow to love math. My eleventh and twelfth grade years, I made 'A's in Algebra II and Algebra III.

The reason I wanted to elaborate on Mr. Jenkins' compassion is because of one of the biggest things he did that I will always remember. My grandmother passed away of cancer during my twelfth grade year. Mr. Jenkins came to her funeral. I didn't even know he was there until he gave me a big hug afterwards and told me everything was going to be okay. I will always remember that because here was my tenth grade teacher concerned about me.

When his son, Lovell Jenkins, Jr. passed away, I went to his funeral to be that backbone for him, like he was for me. I still keep in contact with Mr. Jenkins. He continues to teach at Jefferson Davis, and has since been called to the ministry.

When My Mom Lost Her Job
by
Dashannikia Smith

As a good teacher, one of the most important characteristics is to be a compassionate teacher. One teacher that I remember from elementary school was my 6th grade math teacher. Her name was Mrs. Radcliff and she stands out distinctly in my mind. One of the most distinctive characteristics that I remember about Mrs. Radcliff was her compassion for all of her students. One particular situation that stands out in my mind is when my mom lost her job. I would often feel depressed and subsequently began to fail Mrs. Radcliff's math class. I began to shy away from my friends at school and even became a discipline problem.

Mrs. Radcliff began to notice the problems I was having because I had always done extremely well in her classroom. I remember how compassionate Mrs. Radcliff was about my situation at home and the problems I was having in her class. I remember one day Mrs. Radcliff called me out in the hallway and began to talk to me about the problems I was having in her class. Mrs. Radcliff offered to tutor me twice a week after school to help get my math grade up.

Mrs. Radcliff made me feel that she was very concerned about me. She showed me compassion—even offering to take me home each evening after the tutoring sessions. I really learned that teachers are those who are caring and concerned about their students. I really appreciated Mrs. Radcliff because she was concerned about me. I even began to like math. I truly believe that because of Mrs. Radcliff, I was inspired to become a teacher. Mrs. Radcliff is still teaching 6th grade at Radney Elementary, and I try to go by and visit with her whenever I am in town.

She Made Me Feel Like A Queen
by
Donna E. Freeman

Everyone has a hero or had a hero at some point in his or her life. Whether it's Michael Jordan, Serena Williams, Mayo Angelou, their mother, their father, or even Will Smith, someone has affected us all in our life that has inspired us to believe.

I have many vivid memories of my hero or my role model. Mrs. Cooley was her name. The name of the school was Mattie T. Blount High School. She taught me 10th grade consumer math. She was very intelligent, funny, beautiful, and most of all, compassionate. She expected that all students could and would achieve in her classroom, and she didn't give up on underachievers.

She had lesson plans that gave us (students) a clear idea of what we would be learning, what the assignments were and what the grading policy was. Her assignments had learning goals and gave us (students) ample opportunity to practice new skills. She was very consistent in grading and returned our work in a timely manner. She was in her classroom early and always ready to teach. She presented lessons in a clear and structured way. If someone did not understand what we were working on, she would take her planning period to make sure they understood. Her classroom was organized in such a way as to minimize distractions. I always felt safe in her classroom and she always made me feel secure.

Mrs. Cooley exhibited all the characteristics of an effective teacher, but the one characteristic she exhibited the most was compassion. I have always had a problem with self-esteem, and I recall one incident where Mrs. Cooley made me feel like a queen. This particular day I was feeling like a bum. I hated what I had on. My mother told me she didn't care what I was wearing, just go to school. My whole morning was messed up until I saw Mrs. Cooley. All I could see was her high cheekbones and her pretty white teeth. She knew instantly I was having a bad day. The only thing she said to me was I looked very pretty. She gave me the biggest hug and told me to pass out the papers.

I don't know if she knew it or not, but she made me feel like a queen that day. Mrs. Cooley was the one who inspired me to become a teacher. I have always told myself when I become a teacher; I want to make a difference in all my students' life, just like Mrs. Cooley did in mine.

Wearing Corduroys
by
Andrea Carpenter

I believe that I was very fortunate throughout my elementary, middle and high school years to have several teachers who possessed characteristics of an effective teacher. But, there is one teacher who possessed more characteristics than the others. Her name was Mrs. Martin. She was my fourth grade and sixth grade English teacher. Mrs. Martin was a plump, older woman who looked like the sweetest grandmother in the world.

I am from a very large family. I am the seventh of eight children. My mom and dad worked very hard, but brand name or even new clothes were few and far between. Hand-me-down clothes were a must. I was especially sad one day because I did not like the outfit my mom made me wear to school. I realized that it was very different from the clothes that my friends wore. Sensing my sadness, Mrs. Martin called me out in the hall and told me how pretty I looked that day and that she remembered wearing corduroys as a little girl just like mine. She gave me a huge hug and we returned to the classroom. I realize now that the sadness I felt was very trivial, but the memory of how compassionate Mrs. Martin was that day is one I will never forget.

I could go on for many more pages giving countless examples of how Mrs. Martin was an effective teacher. My goal is that when my students are grown, they will be able to look back and have memories of me as vivid as the ones I have of Mrs. Martin. If I can be half the teacher and person she was, I will reach this goal. She holds a very dear place in my heart, and it is all because she cared enough to be a great teacher.

Having a Really Bad Day
by
Tiffani Bey

My most effective teacher was my seventh grade earth science teacher Dr. Faulkamore. He taught earth science at Penn Wood Jr. High School in Lansdowne, Pennsylvania. Dr. Faulkamore was a white male in his late forties with blonde hair and thick glasses. He looked like the stereotypical science guy you would see in a movie or on a T.V. program. He was very spontaneous and funny. There was never a dull moment when the students came in the classroom.

Dr. Faulkamore made everyone in the class work together. He created an environment where each student had to come up with unique and creative ideas about science. Every Friday we would go outside to the school field and do projects on the earth and its atmosphere. For example, the class would collect a sample of dirt and we would go back into the classroom and examine what we saw under a microscope.

The best characteristic that I would use to describe Dr. Faulkamore would be compassionate. I remember going into the class one day not ready to do anything. I wasn't enthused or happy. I was really having a bad day. Dr. Faulkamore came over to my table and asked me what was wrong, I told him that I was having a really bad day, and didn't feel like doing anything in class today.

An average teacher would have told me to just put my head down or simply do the work, not Dr. Faulkamore. When I told him how I was feeling, he made this weird face and started jumping around really embarrassing himself. I was thinking to myself, "This guy is crazy!" and for him to act the way he did to try to make me feel better was really sweet. I did participate and felt better during the remainder of the class. Even though it was about twenty-eight students in the class, Dr. Faulkamore seem to care about each and every one of us. He was a great teacher that I will never forget.

Menstrual Cycle
by
Karen Sims

As I look back at my educational timeline, I would like to think that I had many effective teachers based on the fact I passed to the next step in my education. I have recently learned the components that make an effective teacher. If these components were looked at closely there is only one teacher, Mrs. Bernadetto, who would measure up to the expectation of being an effective teacher.

Mrs. Bernadetto taught me eighth grade geometry. She was also my softball coach. I had the pleasure of being in Mrs. Bernadetto's sixth period class. I was not that good with geometry but always applied myself. Mrs. Bernadetto always had extreme amounts of patience when it came to helping me work out difficult problems. But I feel the compassion that Mrs. Bernadetto showed is what put her above all the rest.

One instance in particular that stands out was when my menstrual cycle came on for the first time during softball practice. In the process of running around during practice, I did not realize this was happening to me. By the time practice was over, my clothes were soaked. While the other girls laughed, Mrs. Bernadetto calmed me down and got me another pair of sweats to wear. While Mrs. Bernadetto could not stop the girls from laughing at me, she did make me feel comfortable enough to return to school the next day.

Mrs. Bernadetto had the compassion that most teachers need in today's classroom. By Mrs. Bernadetto showing concern for me, it made an otherwise embarrassing disaster bearable.

My Angel
by
Phelecya Ivey

I would like to tell you about the best teacher in the world in my eyes. She was a gift from God. I did not always think these wonderful things about her. She really had to grow on me. In the beginning of the school year, I did not like Mrs. Jackson very much. She was my 6th grade homeroom English teacher. Mrs. Jackson had been a teacher at Arrington Middle School located in Birmingham, Alabama for over 30 years when I became a student in her class.

Every morning when we entered Mrs. Jackson's class, she would always have the same speech about when we went to our other teachers' classes that we would be representing her. I laughed because I thought it was funny. After the speech, she would go over or explain the lessons thoroughly and she gave us homework every night. Mrs. Jackson always made me sit in the front of the class because I would always talk when she was teaching the class. She gave me detention and Saturday school almost every day for being disruptive in the hallways, being out of uniform, and writing on the bathroom walls. I could not stand Mrs. Jackson! I thought she was the meanest person in the world! This is what really made me not like her—she would make us wear a gigantic piece of paper with our name written in big red letters if we did not wear our I.D. everyday. All of the other students would laugh and make jokes about my class. I can admit that she was a good teacher. But all the mean things made me overlook the good side of her.

I remember one incident that made me change the way I felt about Mrs. Jackson. It was about 6:00 a.m. in the morning. I was awakened by loud shouting and black smoke. My house was on fire! I was so terrified! I started crying and panicking.

Even though the fire station was down the street, it took the firemen about 30 minutes to get to the house. By that time, my home had suffered major fire damage. Everyone who passed my house on their way to school witnessed the horrible disaster.

To this day, I still remember Mrs. Jackson pulling into my driveway. She got out of her car and came and gave me a hug. She said that everything would be okay. From that day on, I had the utmost respect for Mrs. Jackson.

I was out of school for about two weeks. Mrs. Jackson found out where I was staying and brought me my school work so that I would not be behind. On top of that, she raised money for my family and me. That was a great feeling.

When I returned to school there were cards, balloons, pizza, soda, chips, and music waiting for me in the classroom. I was overjoyed. I started crying. I knew from that day on that Mrs. Jackson was the most compassionate person I had ever met. Even now I still go by and visit Mrs. Jackson. She is now retired. Each time I get a chance to be around Mrs. Jackson, I tell her that she made a difference in my life. Mrs. Jackson is one of the main reasons I chose teaching as a profession. I am working hard so that I can one day have the same impact on a student.

G.I. Joe Dad
by
Sandra Matthews-Staley

Growing up in a country town, many children were treated differently due to their race, nationality and religion. I was fortunate to have a loving teacher in kindergarten, Mrs. Betty Jean Kliss. Mrs Kliss had taught kindergarten for over 40 years. She had several characteristics of an effective teacher. Being compassionate was just one of many that stood out.

One incident that I remember as clear as day, was around Labor Day. The students were asked to tell about their parents occupations, and it was not uncommon for many of the students' mothers to be stay-at-home moms. I was okay with that part, because my mother was also a stay-at-home mom and she would often volunteer to help Mrs. Kliss. So, my mother was a special parent for being active in our classroom. But when I was asked by another student, what my father's occupation was, I became embarrassed and upset because my father died when I was 16 months old and I really didn't know him.

Mrs. Kliss had known a lot about my family background, because she and my mother communicated often. Mrs. Kliss explained to the class that my father was in the U.S. Army and had served in the Vietnam War. Of course many of us didn't know what that meant, but the word "War" stood out in the minds of many of the kindergartners.

During this time the G.I. Joe figurines were popular with the boys and they were all excited to know that my daddy was in the Army. Once again, Mrs. Kliss made me feel proud to be the daughter of a veteran even though I could not remember him. She asked me to bring pictures of my dad taken when he was in Vietnam to share with the class. And you know I was happy to show off those pictures with my dad holding his gun, sitting in a tent, riding on a jeep and wearing face paint. This event was a profound and lasting memory that I have of Mrs. Kliss' compassion that has affected me positively.

She Made Me Feel Safe
by
Demetress Yvette Wood

When I think about my most effective elementary school teacher, I think about Kathryn Davis. Mrs. Davis was my third grade Language Arts teacher at

Charles Dickens Elementary School in Cleveland, Ohio. All of the students at Charles Dickens Elementary School loved Mrs. Davis. I feel that Mrs. Davis was an effective teacher because she was kind, sincere, and enthusiastic. She seemed to genuinely care about her students. She also displayed a deep sincere love for teaching.

There are several other reasons why Mrs. Davis sticks out in my mind. First, she introduced me to different types of music and gave me an appreciation of poetry. In our class, she would play different types of music such as classical, slow, sad, and upbeat. She would turn off the lights in class and tell us to close our eyes and visualize a story or a poem by listening to the music. After we finished listening to the music, we would write our own individual story or poem. This activity for writing has stayed with me. Whenever I have to write long essays or research papers, I will turn on some jazz music, relax my mind and let the thoughts flow. After I took Mrs. Davis' class, I started writing short stories and poems in a journal. I kept doing this activity until I graduated from high school.

The second and most important reason why I remember Mrs. Davis is because of her compassion. Out of all of the 12 characteristics of an effective teacher, Mrs. Davis' compassion toward me stands out. I will never forget that cold day in March, when my mother came and checked my cousin and me out of school. I could tell that something was wrong but I just did not know what it was. My mother took my cousin Eric and me to her friends house. Later my uncle showed up and gave my cousin Eric the bad news. My Aunt Carol, Eric's mother, had been murdered. I remember the days and weeks that followed were filled with grief, anger and shock. We were taken out of school for about two weeks. We had to go to Alabama to bury Aunt Carol.

During that time, everything seemed like a blur, it was not real. When we were back at home and in school again, I began to have problems. I would cry in class and I remember feeling afraid all the time. Mrs. Davis would take me out of class and talk to me. She would tell me that everything was going to be okay, and she would always hug me. I remember that she made me feel safe. Mrs. Davis also visited my mother and me at our home. She brought my schoolwork and helped me to catch up on my missed assignments.

I have had other teachers throughout high school and college who have influenced me and gave me a zest for learning. However, Mrs. Kathryn Davis was the most influential and effective teacher I ever had. I do not know what has happened to Mrs. Davis. One of my elementary school classmates told me that Mrs. Davis and her husband had moved to Texas. The last time I saw her, I was in the seventh grade. I remember her giving me a pep talk about being a good student and going on to college.

She Taught Me How To Love
by
Ursula Goldsmith

What makes an effective teacher? Some teachers have many qualities that make them effective. However, to help clarify my position, I believe it would be befitting for me to explain what made my fourth grade teacher effective. When you're effective, the students learn, enjoy class, and feel comfortable expressing themselves, but most importantly, an effective teacher is compassionate.

Compassion is a term that describes my fourth grade teacher, Mrs. Rhuhalmia Young. Mrs. Young taught social studies and science (my favorite subjects). Webster defines compassion as having empathy and a deep, sincere, and long standing sympathy for someone suffering or distress in some way. Compassion is a characteristic that is sincere, in that your actions speak louder than words.

At the age of ten, during my fourth grade year in school, my mother died in a car accident one Friday night. I can remember that following afternoon, Mrs. Young and several other teachers came to visit my sister and me. Although several teachers visited that day, it was Mrs. Young that came by everyday thereafter for weeks. After this tragedy in my family, she was always there trying to make me feel loved and important.

Another example of her compassion is that she never forgot about me. She followed my education until I completed high school. She let me know that she would always be there for me. Even now, she remembers me when we meet around town.

In conclusion, this is one of the characteristics that made her an exemplary teacher. A compassionate teacher addresses the whole student and not a portion. Education should cover a variety of aspect in a student's life, with learning being the main focus. She didn't just instill knowledge in me, but she also taught me how to love and care for others.

A Little Something Extra At Christmas
by
Shelia A. Usen

The effective teacher I had in elementary school was Mrs. Thomas. My mother worked two jobs at the time, and I was the youngest of six children. I had to pretty much take care of myself starting at a young age. I also had a lazy tongue. Mrs. Thomas would remind me whenever I mispronounced a word that I was not pronouncing it right. She would make me look at her mouth whenever I mispronounced a word, so that she could demonstrate how to pronounce the word correctly. I do not fault my mother, because as a single parent, she had to make tough choices in order to care for her six children by herself.

Nevertheless, Mrs. Thomas filled a lot of voids in my life that my mother could not provide (though she wanted to). When I would act out in school,

Mrs. Thomas would discipline me; then later in the evening, after school, she would phone my mother to inform her of my disruptive acts in class. Of course, my mother would thank her and proceed to discipline me again for acting out in school.

That particular year, my mother was hospitalized for a short while, so she missed work. Unfortunately, it was Christmas time. On the last day before the Christmas break, Mrs. Thomas brought gifts to all of her students. However, she stuck a little something extra in my bag because she knew of my mother's financial troubles. Mrs. Thomas stepped in and did what she could to encourage me and to help my family. Because of the compassionate way Mrs. Thomas treated me, I knew I was special to her and was loved by her.

Summary

This book shared with you stories of inspiring teachers who were successful in getting their students to behave appropriately and to learn the subject matter. It presented heartwarming stores of teachers who saw teaching not as a job, but as a noble mission—as a ministry. This book spoke of teachers who made a difference in the lives of their students and were what inspired these students to also become teachers.

What started out as a simple first week class assignment evolved into an educational revelation. Over my collegiate teaching career, I engaged college students in discussions and writing assignments pertaining to the outstanding characteristics of their most effective teacher. Effective was defined as that teacher who made the most significant impact on their lives. Students consistently identified similar qualities among highly effective teachers.

After years of listening to students speak about their favorite and most memorable teachers, and after years of reading students' essays on the topic, the following 12 characteristics of an effective teacher were identified:

(1) Prepared
(2) Positive
(3) High Expectations
(4) Creative
(5) Fair
(6) Personal Touch
(7) Develops a Sense of Belonging
(8) Admits Mistakes
(9) Sense of Humor
(10) Gives Respect to Students
(11) Forgiving
(12) Compassionate

What is so significant about this discovery is the fact that these characteristics are more personal traits than they are academic traits. Consequently, these are not qualities you can learn by going through a college academic course of study or by way of a textbook. These characteristics are developed by loving children and building a relationship with them.

Throughout the pages of this book, you have been challenged to develop a new way of thinking about your role as a teacher. You can no longer view yourself as merely a dispenser of knowledge.

Hopefully, through reading this volume, you have come to realize that your greatest responsibility in teaching children is not the imparting of book knowledge, but the building of character—and the best way to build character is by example.

This book presented true stories written by Education majors as they recounted their experiences of being taught (grades K-12) by an effective teacher. It shared actual classroom examples of teachers who manifested each of the 12 Characteristics of an Effective Teacher.

For those of you who have been teaching for a number of years and are now facing the possibility of burnout—I hope that the essays presented served to rejuvenate you and reminded you of the reason you chose teaching as a profession—to make a difference in the lives of children.

I am a product of and a firm advocate of public education. With all the things children have to face in today's society, now, more than ever, children need loving and caring public school teachers. Many of the children we teach come from dysfunctional homes. Many have no religious upbringing. They do not regularly attend a church, synagogue, mosque, temple, or any place of worship where the principles of right and wrong are being taught. For many children, coming to public school is the only positive thing happening in their lives. It is their last best hope! As public school teachers, if we don't love them, care for them, and give them the proper guidance, then, please tell me, who will? Even the most rebellious and hard-hearted child will change when he knows he is loved.

***

Acquiring the 12 Characteristics of an Effective Teacher really boils down to treating the children in your classroom the way you want to be treated; or more importantly—the way you would want your own child to be treated. Ask yourself, are you the type of teacher you would want teaching *your* child?

By acquiring these 12 characteristics, you can have a positive impact on the lives of the children you teach. In order to change the lives of children, you must model those characteristics you seek to instill in the hearts and minds of the children you teach. Changing lives is the true essence of the ***12 Characteristics of an Effective Teacher.***

"Train up a child in the way he should go: and when he is old, he will not depart from it" *(Proverbs 22:6).*

About the author:
Dr. Robert J. Walker is an assistant professor in the College of Education, Department of Curriculum and Instruction, at Alabama State University, Montgomery, Alabama. He is a volunteer math tutor at E. D. Nixon Elementary and a volunteer computer technician at Bethany Christian Academy. He is a member of the National Education Association (NEA) and the Alabama Education Association (AEA).

Works Cited

1. (Prepared)

Renard, Lisa. "What to Do! What to Do!" *ASCD's Classroom Leadership Online*, Vol. 2 Number 8: 1999.

Wong, Harry K & Rosemary T. Wong. *How to Be An Effective Teacher: The First Days Of School*. Mountain View, California: Harry K. Wong Publications, Inc., 2001.

2. (Positive)

Haynes, Judie. "Creating an Atmosphere of Acceptance." *http://www.everythingESL.net*. 1998-2004.

3. (High Expectations)

Gazin, Ann. "What Do You Expect?" *Instructor*, 2004.

Wong, Harry K & Rosemary T. Wong. *How to Be An Effective Teacher: The First Days Of School.* Mountain View, California: Harry K. Wong Publications, Inc., 2001.

4. (Creativity)

Baltz, Pann. *Creativity in the Classroom: An Exploration. The Creative Classroom Project.* Project Zero, Harvard Graduate School of Education, 124 Mount Auburn Street, Fifth Floor, Cambridge, MA 02138,

Manzo, Anthony and Ula. "Teaching Children to Be Literate: A Reflective Approach." *Instructional Elements for Fostering Higher-Order Thinking in the Classroom*, 1995.

5. (Fair)

Paul, David. "Getting Down to Basics: Gaining Respect from Children in the Classroom." *The Daily Yomiuri*, 2002.

Salzmann, Mary E. *I Am Fair*. Minnesota: Sand Castle, 2002.

6. (Personal Touch)

Sadker, Myra & David. "Classroom Tips for Non-Sexist, Non-Racist Teaching." *Teachers, Schools & Society*. McGraw Hill, 2005.

7. (Developing a Sense of Belonging)

Brick, Madeline. "Increase Students' Sense of Belonging with Responsive Classroom Philosophy: An Interview with Madeline," *Curriculum Review*, 2002.

Smith, Denise. "Inclusion Education." *Fuerstenau Early Childhood Center*, 2004.

8. (Admits to Mistakes)

Costa, Arthur L. & Bena Kallick. "Remaining Open to Continuous Learning." http://www.habits-of-mind.net. 2004.

Walters, Stephanie. "What do I when I realize I've made a mistake with a child?" http://www .rethinkingschools.org/publication/newteacher/NTQA2. shtml, 2004.

9. (Sense of Humor)

Girdlefanny, Snotty. "Using Humor in the Classroom." *Techniques,* 2005.

Lipman, Larry. "Humor & Fun in Team Building and the Classroom." *Fun Team Building,* 2004.

10. (Giving Respect to Students)

Court T.V. "Respecting Young Adolescents." *A Teacher's Guide: Working with Young Adolescents*, 2005.

Ritzer, Darren R & Merry J. Sleigh. "Encouraging Student Attendance." *American Psychological Society*, 2001.

11. (Forgiving)

Sams, Tim. "The Art of Forgiveness." *My Sacred Journey,* 2004.

Wiednhoff, Filiann. "Tips and advice to help you forgive" –Dealing with Un-Forgiveness and Ditterness Release it and Let it Go - *Helium Religion & Spirituality.* http://www.helium.com/items/809613-dealing-forgiveness-bitterness-release

Wright, Rusty. "Forgiveness Can Be Good for Your Health." http://www.probe.org/docs/forgive.html, 2000.

12. (Compassionate)

Raatma, Lucia. Caring. Minnesota: Capstone Press, 2000.

Wong, Harry K & Rosemary T. Wong. *How to Be An Effective Teacher: The First Days Of School.* Mountain View, California: Harry K. Wong Publications, Inc., 2001.

Bibliography

Amrein-Beardsley, A. (September 2007), "Recruiting Expert Teachers into Hard-to-Staff Schools," Phi Delta Kappa International. Phi Delta Kappan, v89 n1 p64 67 Web site: http://www.pdkintl.org/publications/pubshome.htm

Adams, C.M. and Pierce, R.L. "Characteristics of Effective Teaching." www.bsu.edu/gradschool/media/pdf/chapter12.pdf . (download from internet 2008)

Babyak, A. E., Luze, G. J., and Kamps, D. B. (March 2000). "The Good Student Game: Behavior Management for Diverse Class rooms." *Intervention in School and Clinic* 35(4):216-223.

Banach, W. J. (2007). *The ABCs of Teacher-Parent Communication.* Rowman & Littlefield Education.

Barr, A. S. (1929). *Characteristic Differences in the Teaching Performance of Good and Poor Teachers of the Social Studies.* University of Wisconsin Public School Publishing Company. Bloomington, Illinois. Digital formatted October 8, 2007.

Bailey, D. L., and Helms, R. G. (2000). *The National Board Certified Teacher.* Fastback 470. Bloomington, IN: Phi Delta Kappa Educational Foundation.

Bicard, D. F. (May 2000). "Using Classroom Rules to Construct Behavior." *Middle School Journal* 31 (5):37-45.

Brown, K. E. and Medway, F. J. (May 2007). "School Climate and Teacher Beliefs in a School Effectively Serving Poor South Carolina (USA) African-American Students: A Case Study." *Teaching and Teacher Education: An International Journal of Research and Studies*, v23 n4 p529-540.

Case, R. L. (Fall 2002). "Not Separate but Not Equal: How Should the United States Address Its International Obligations to Eradicate Racial Discrimination in the Public Education System?" 21 Penn State International Law Review 205-226, 215-226 (136 Footnotes)

"Characteristics of Effective Teaching." (download from internet 2008 spectrum.troy.edu/~mjparker/eff_teach.htm)

Cornell, C. (Summer 1999). "I Hate Math I Couldn't Learn It, and I Can't Teach It!" *Childhood Education* 75(4):225-230.

Crimmins, D. and Farrell, A. F. (2007). *Positive Strategies for Students with Behavior Problems* Brookes Publishing Company.

Curwin, R L., and Mendler, A. N. (1999). *As Tough as Necessary: Countering Aggression, Violence, and Hostility in Schools.* Alexandria, VA: Association for Supervision and Curriculum Development.

Danielson, C. (1996). *Enhancing Professional Practice: A Framework for Teaching* Alexandria, VA: Association for Supervision and Curriculum Development.

DiGiulio, R. (2000). *Positive Classroom Management.* 2d ed. Thousand Oaks, CA: Corwin.

Duncan-Andrade, J. (November 2007). "Gangstas, Wankstas, and Ridas: Defining, Developing, and Supporting Effective Teachers in Urban Schools." *International Journal of Qualitative Studies in Education (QSE),* v20 n6 p617-638. Edwards, C. H. (Spring 2000). "The Moral Dimension of Teaching and Classroom Discipline." *American Secondary Education* 28(S):20-25.

Freiberg, H. J. (1999). *Beyond Behaviorism: Changing the Classroom Management Paradigm.* Needhain Heights, MA: Allyn & Bacon.

Freiberg, H. J. (1999). *Perceiving, Behaving, Becoming: Lessons Learned.* Alexandria, VA: Association for Supervision and Curriculum Development.

Gold, J. M., Rotter, J. C., Holmes, G. R., and Motes, P. S. (1999). *Middle School Climate: A Study of Attitudes.* Fastback 455. Bloomington, IN: Phi Delta Kappa Educational Foundation,

Gootman, M. F. (2001). *The Caring Teacher's Guide to Discipline: Helping Young Students Learn Self-Control, Responsibility, and Respect.* 2d ed. Thousand Oaks, CA: Corwin Press.

Hepburn, S. L. and DiGuiseppi, C. (February 2008). "Use of a Teacher Nomination Strategy to Screen for Autism Spectrum Disorders in General Education Classrooms: A Pilot Study." *Journal of Autism and Developmental Disorders,* v38 n2 p373-382.

Hodgkinson, H. (December 2000/January 2001). "Educational Demographics: What Teachers Should Know," *Educational Leadership* 58(4) 6-11.

Johnson, L. E. and Reiman, A. J. (July 2007). "Beginning Teacher Disposition: Examining the Moral/Ethical Domain." *Teaching and Teacher Education:* An International Journal of Research and Studies, v23 n5 p676-687.

Lacina, J. and Watson, P. (Spring 2008). "A Focus on Literacy: Effective Content Teachers for the Middle Grades." *Childhood Education,* v84 n3 p159.

Linkous, V. (Spring 2000). "Simply Speaking. Issues in Education." *Childhood Education* 76(3):161.

McKinney, S. E. and Haberman, M. (2008). "Developing Teachers for High-Poverty Schools: The Role of the Internship Experience." *Urban Education*, v43 n1 p68-82.

Onwuegbuzie, A.J. and Witcher, A. E.; (2007). "Students' Perceptions of Characteristics of Effective College Teachers: A Validity Study of a Teaching Evaluation Form Using a Mixed-Methods Analysis." *American Educational Research Journal*, v44 n1 p113-160

Park, G.; Lee, H. (2006). "The Characteristics of Effective English Teachers as Perceived by High School Teachers and Students in Korea." *Asia Pacific Education Review*, v7 n2 p236-248

Poland, S. (March 2000). "The Fourth R—Relationships." *American School Board Journal* 187(3)45-46

Polk, J. A. (Mar-Apr 2006). "Traits of Effective Teachers." *Arts Education Policy Review*. v107 n4 p23-29.

Rea, D., Millican, K. P., and Watson, S. W. (March 2000). "The Serious Benefits of Fun in the Classroom." *Middle School Journal* 31(4):23-28

Rushton, S., Morgan, J. and Richard, M. (May 2007). "Teacher's Myers-Briggs Personality Profiles: Identifying Effective Teacher Personality Traits." *Teaching and Teacher Education: An International Journal of Research and Studies*, v23 n4 p432-441.

Smerdon, B. A., Burkan, D. T., and Lee, V. E. (Fall 1999). "Access to Constructivist and Didactic Teaching: Who Gets It? Where Is It Practiced?" *Teachers College Record* 101 (1) :5-34.

Somech, A.and Ron, I. (2007). "Promoting Organizational Citizenship Behavior in Schools: The Impact of Individual and Organizational Characteristics." *Educational Administration Quarterly*, v43 n1 p38-66.

Stodolsky, S. S., and Grossman, P. L. (February 2000). "Changing Student, Changing Teaching." *Teachers College Record* 102(1):125-172

Tedford, J. (January 2008). "Collecting Best Practices." *Principal Leadership*, v8 n5 p27-30

Virtue, D.C. (May-June 2007) "Teaching and Learning in the Middle Grades: A Personal Perspective." *Clearing House:* A Journal of Educational Strategies, Issues and Ideas, v80 n5 p243-244.

Wasley P. (May 1999). "Teaching Worth Celebrating." *Educational Leadership* 56(8) :8-13

Wassermann, S. (February 1999). "Shazam! You're a Teacher." *Phi Delta Kappan* 80(6):464, 466-468.

Wong, H. K. and T. Wong, R.T. (2001).*How to Be An Effective Teacher: The First Days Of School.*_Mountain View, California: Harry K. Wong Publications, Inc.,

Index

CPSIA information can be obtained at www.ICGtesting.com
Printed in the USA
237060LV00005B/159/P